CW00972133

TheRevolutionofMoney.com

Paperback: 9798884867512
Hardcover: 9798884869974

ACKNOWLEDGEMENTS

This book would not have been possible without the support and encouragement from a group of remarkable individuals to whom we owe our gratitude.

First and foremost, we would like to thank our family for their input and unwavering support throughout this process.

Special thanks to Omid Malekan, whose guidance was indispensable, and to our friends (you know who you are), for their invaluable feedback and encouragement.

We appreciate the professional input and expertise of former colleagues, particularly those at Galaxy Digital, who significantly contributed to the refinement of this work.

Finally, we extend our thanks to the readers, who are the ultimate reason this book exists.

To all mentioned, and to those unnamed who contributed in various ways, thank you.

DISCLAIMER

This book aims to introduce fundamental ideas about money in an accessible and engaging manner, making the subject approachable for readers of all backgrounds.

It is important to note that this book is not an exhaustive resource on all financial topics. In the pursuit of clarity and simplicity, certain complex or specialized subjects have been simplified or omitted. These include, but are not limited to, topics such as fractional reserve banking, quantitative easing, the underlying mechanics of bonds, and proof-of-work blockchains.

Readers seeking a deeper or more technical understanding of these areas are encouraged to consult our website, TheRevolutionofMoney.com, which includes a resource library. This book should be viewed as a starting point for thinking critically about money and its importance rather than a comprehensive guide to every aspect of the field.

CONTENTS

FOREWORD

Money is all around us. Money is in our pockets, in our stores, on our screens. Everything man-made you interact with was produced for money, contains components that were purchased with money, made by someone who was paid in money. The food you eat was grown for money on land purchased for money. The streets you drive upon were paved for money, the lights operate on electricity that costs money, and your town is designed by a city planner paid with tax money. People literally say "time is money." There are very few things in our world that have no relation to money.

But what is money? Is it an invention? Is it a technology? Is it natural? Where does money come from? How is money created, and by whom? How does money get from creation to circulation? Does the bank have the money? Is it in a vault somewhere? Why is money valuable, and some monies more valuable than others?

These are fundamental questions about a ubiquitous phenomenon that many people never ask. I didn't ask these questions until my late 20s. Like most people, I just accepted money's existence and value as an inherent feature of our world. But when you start asking these questions, you discover that money is a lot more interesting and its history much more curious—and evolving—than you ever knew.

If you are asking yourself these questions, and have wondered why money is the way it is, you are reading the right book. Sam and Ben Baker masterfully and concisely explain the phenomenon of money: its purpose, its value, its history, its future.

Now is a perfect time to learn about the nature of money. Since the COVID-19 pandemic, inflation has raged around the world, reducing the value of money. The causes of this inflation are complex, but one of the primary drivers was that governments and central banks printed enormous amounts of money in a bid to support the ravaged economy by paying the citizenry. It turns out that creating a LOT of something tends to make the value of individual items less valuable. Scarcity is a key driver in the value of goods; a rare trading card is worth more than a common one, gold is worth more than silver, etc. Businesses often introduce artificial scarcity to drive engagement and sales ("limited time only!"). When things become LESS scarce, they often become less valuable.

Sam and Ben Baker diligently and entertainingly tell the history of money's emergence in ancient times. And it did EMERGE; the evidence shows that money is genuinely a fundamental emerging phenomenon likely to appear and evolve in ANY society of intelligent beings. Initial monies were always scarce commodities found in nature: shells that were available but still scarce; stones that were mineable but still difficult to mine; animals that were useful but took effort to raise, etc. The best money has always had this key property: the ability to be produced at scale but with difficulty. Gold coins were the iconic currency of the world's advanced civilizations as early as the Lydian Kings, and one of the main reasons that gold emerged as a powerful money was that it exists all over the world, but it's still hard to find and mine, making it scarce, but not TOO scarce.

But we don't use gold today. We use fiat currency—that is, money willed into existence by decree of the government and central banks. And herein lies a serious problem. The history of money contains myriad examples of scarcity manipulation. When the Romans sought to devalue their coins (i.e., inflate the money supply) they literally had to make new coins with lower gold composition and introduce them into the economy. But with fiat money, central bankers can push a few buttons and create money out of thin air. Indeed, the manipulation of the money supply is so common that it is actually the primary function of the world's central banks. Tinkering with the value of our money is business-as-usual for the central bank. The Federal Reserve has 23,000 employees in the United States and every single one wakes up every day to contribute to the work of tinkering with the supply of US dollars.

History is very long. Much has happened—and then happened again. People forget and instead think that modern society is different than the past. The status quo always wants you to believe that history has reached an apex, that no further innovations are needed, that everything has been figured out. The system doesn't need updating. The dollar will always be the world's reserve currency. It can't possibly be that someone invented a new type of money after thousands of years.

But the reality is that history is longer than you think, and not everything has been "figured out." Indeed, it is very possible for something like Bitcoin to emerge and become a force—to really matter. Indeed, it has. What will be the money of tomorrow? Sam and Ben Baker think it might be Bitcoin, and they might be right.

Alex Thorn

INTRODUCTION

In the heart of the Sunbelt, amidst a dusty field surrounded by guard towers, a group of orange-clad men engage in a spirited game of pickup football. This scene unfolds within the confines of a state penitentiary where inmates spend their yard time immersed in the quintessential American pastime. However, for Dr. Gibson-Light, an Associate Professor of Sociology and Criminology, the real intrigue lies not in the game itself, but in the group of men on the sidelines. Deeply engrossed in the game, these observers pass packets of ramen back and forth after noteworthy plays on the field. A touchdown is scored, and a young man begrudgingly hands over his precious noodles to a wide-eyed old-timer. The game ends, and a flurry of noodles changes hands as the inmates settle the final score.

This was a form of gambling, a "workplace football pool" within the prison walls, where ramen noodles took the place of dollar bills. Dr. Gibson-Light's extensive research, spanning 18 months of ethnographic fieldwork in a men's state prison, uncovered the widespread use of ramen noodles as the de facto currency. The prison harbored a surprisingly intricate economy where inmates traded ramen noodles for various goods and services, from food and clothing to collectibles and luxury items. The costs varied: two packets for a sweatshirt, four for a bag of coffee beans, and six for a pair of thermals, to name a few transactions.

This study highlights the prevalence of informal monetary systems within the harsh confines of prison environments. In a telling field interview, an inmate explained the significance of ramen, stating, "You can gauge a man's [financial] well-being by the number of soups in his locker. 'Twenty soups? That guy's doing well!' It's like the outside world—currency is essential for everything. Here, it's all about the soups."[1]

Several hundred miles to the south, Richard Davies, a noted research economist and author, uncovers a similar economic phenomenon within the Louisiana State Penitentiary. Often referred to as the "Alcatraz of the South," this maximum-security facility sprawls over 18,000 acres—a landmass surpassing the island of Manhattan in size—and confines approximately 5,200 inmates. The environment is daunting, with an average sentence of 92 years, resulting in around 70% of inmates facing the reality of life behind bars. To call this environment hostile would be an understatement.

Despite housing some of the nation's most hardened criminals, the Louisiana State Penitentiary also hosts a bustling underground economy similar to the one observed in Dr. Gibson-Light's study. Inmates seeking grooming services or freshly pressed shirts find their needs met through an informal network of services provided by fellow prisoners, who run a host of informal businesses that the guards turn a blind eye to. One prisoner prides himself on his impeccable pecan pralines, reminiscent of his birthplace in the deep South. Another cooks the best fried chicken the prisoners have ever tasted (within a penitentiary, of course). Cigarettes fuel this entire underground economy instead of ramen noodles as the preferred medium of exchange; even inmates who do not smoke need to acquire and keep a stock of tobacco because they understand the simple fact that tobacco serves as the universal form of payment in the facility.

A broader view of correctional facilities across the United States and globally uncovers a startling reality: The use of ramen noodles and cigarettes as makeshift currencies is not an isolated phenomenon. In various American prisons, emergent commodity markets spring up around all sorts of precious goods. Some populations choose postage stamps and canned mackerel as their alternative currencies. Across the pond, at prisons in the UK, shower gels and rolling papers emerge as the currencies of choice.

While the inner workings of prison economics may appear random, as Davies notes, "That the extremes of life offer important lessons is an idea widely used by scientists."[2] In the case of money, the presence of ramen-noodle and cigarette currency in prison economies helps reveal the answer to two fundamental questions: **How does money emerge within society, and more importantly, *why* does it emerge?**

A new observer might be quick to ask: "Why don't prisoners simply use regular cash, as people do in the outside world?" The answer lies in the complex dynamics of prison life. In these environments, hard cash is regarded as a significant contraband item. Dollars are the gateway to the outside world, for they can be used to bribe prison guards for favors, smuggled goods, or potentially a means of escape. It is no surprise, therefore, that even the most hardened criminals are afraid of carrying even a small amount of cash.

One might also expect simple systems of barter to form within the prison, with one prisoner giving up his unwanted cans of mackerel in exchange for a coveted bottle of shampoo. While such direct exchanges do occur, they often face a logistical hurdle: the challenge of finding someone who not only has the item you desire but also wants what you're offering in return. This phenomenon is formally called the "double coincidence of wants," a term initially coined by the famed economist William Stanley Jevons in his 1875 book *Money and the Mechanism of Exchange*.

To understand the practical limitations of barter, imagine this hypothetical scenario: Charlie, an inmate within the Louisiana State Penitentiary, loves to treat himself to a cup of watery coffee whenever he can get his hands on coffee grounds. Charlie also loathes lentils, which unfortunately appear in his daily food rations. Some inmates who receive coffee from their families are willing to trade for lentils. However, the timing is often misaligned: When Charlie has lentils, the other inmates might not have coffee. If Charlie gives lentils in hopes of getting coffee later, he risks not being repaid, as he doesn't trust these inmates completely. Alternatively, he would owe a debt if he asked for coffee first and promised lentils later. Debts in prisons are notoriously dangerous; it is not uncommon for a prisoner to be severely beaten or even killed over an outstanding debt of just a few ramen packets.

At the core of this thought experiment lies a fundamental problem of trust: For Charlie to solve the barter problem, he must be willing to trust that every prisoner he trades with will pay him back in the future, or conversely, they must place trust in him that he will pay back his debt. In prisons, it can take years to build up the confidence needed to coordinate such a trade, with the slightest of infractions having the potential to shatter any trust built up.

Thus, the usage of ramen noodles and cigarettes emerges as a tool to solve the trust problem. These precious commodities are high enough in demand that while it may be hard to find a prisoner willing to take Charlie's lentils, any prisoner with coffee would gladly accept cigarettes or ramen at the right price.

While the adoption of cigarette currency in the Louisiana State Penitentiary might seem insignificant, the emergence of monies in early human societies followed an identical process. Just as cigarettes solve the problems of barter and trust in prison systems, so too did early monies such as shells and gold coins. For early humans, money proved to be an invaluable technology that empowered cooperation and trade in ways that were otherwise impossible. The utility of money is even more apparent today, serving as the foundation of our eight billion-person economy.

One of the core messages of this book is that money is one of the most important yet misunderstood technologies in our lives. Understanding the evolution of money is foundational to grasping how our system works.

The first part of this book will explore the emergence and importance of money in early human societies, from the dawn of hunter-gatherers until the height of the pre-industrial era. This exploration examines the reasons *why* money initially emerged and the conditions that shaped its evolution to build a framework for understanding how money enables civilization to scale.

Using this framework, the second part of the book explores the pivotal developments and events that shaped the money of today, which took on its present form in the year 1971 and has since damaged the proper functioning of the economy and society.

In 1971, President Richard Nixon took a historic step by decoupling the dollar from its gold backing. This decision marked the first instance in history where the world's reserve currency lacked a natural, physical constraint, giving the United States the unprecedented ability to spend and accumulate debt without restraint. As a result, the US dollar became more susceptible to political influences and less tethered to real-world economic activities, marking a significant departure from money's traditional role in the global economy.

Formerly a monetary tool serving the broader welfare of society, today's money is the linchpin of a complex financial system heavily reliant on debt and leverage, as will be explored in part two of the book. The downstream effects of this decision have been nothing short of profound. Before 1971, the United States was an export powerhouse with a robust manufacturing base. Since then, American businesses and blue-collar jobs have been offshored, leaving the US with a chronic trade imbalance (shown below).[3]

The United States' balance of trade since the 1960s. Since 1971, the US has had a chronic negative balance, meaning it imports more goods and services than it exports.[3]

The year 1971 also marked the beginning of a multitude of damaging trends, including a widening of income inequality, an untethering of housing affordability from incomes, and a rapid rise in our nation's debt—now exceeding $34 trillion, more than $100,000 per American citizen.[3]

Income Gains Have Not Been Shared Since 1971

Growth in US Home Prices Outpaces Incomes

(Top) Since 1971, the top 20% of US families have seen a far greater rise in their incomes than the middle and bottom 20%, representing an increase in income inequality (Nominal income normalized to 100 in 1971).[4] (Bottom) Since 1971, US home prices have increased far faster than family incomes.[3]

Federal Budget Surplus/Deficit

Since 1971, the US federal budget deficit went from non-existent to deeply in the negative by 2020.[3]

Understanding this shift helps explain the loss of trust in American institutions and our increasingly polarized political climate. Despite differing political perspectives, concerns raised by both the political right and left are in response to systemic issues rooted in this shared fundamental change.

Part two of this book combines these lessons of history with the reasoning of the brightest economic thinkers of our time and provides an explanation for why all these trends proliferated. Readers can expect to gain an understanding of the current US dollar system, why it was formed, and how it no longer serves the American people as intended.

Lastly, part three explores how technological progress can now enable money to effectively serve our deeply interconnected, global, and digital society. In this context, cryptocurrency—specifically Bitcoin—emerges as a compelling solution, offering a modern approach to money that addresses what went wrong in 1971. The motivation behind this book is rooted in the belief that Bitcoin's widespread adoption is not only likely but also pivotal in addressing these growing concerns.

Just as we took a skeptical yet curious approach to researching for this book, we encourage readers to do the same. Question the assumptions that you have held about economics and money. Do your own research. Come to your own conclusions. In doing so, we collectively are bound to move toward a more prosperous future.

PART I

MONEY OF THE PAST

CHAPTER 1

THE EVOLUTION OF COOPERATION

The origins of money and its pivotal role in civilization's progression are best understood by exploring an era 38,000 years before the present day, predating the agricultural revolution by 10,000 years. During this era, small bands of nomadic hunters traversed vast expanses of the globe, having descended from groups that migrated from Africa and the Fertile Crescent in earlier millennia. Clad in furs, armed with basic spears and blunt tools for hunting, these nomads often carried their belongings on their backs. Among these primitive possessions was something of far greater significance: intricately crafted necklaces of cowrie shells adorning their necks and wrists.

The craftsmanship of this shell-made jewelry was far from primitive. The cowrie shells were meticulously selected and shaped into dazzling displays of wealth. Evidence of these ornate shells is widespread: Shells dating to as early as 73,000 BCE were unearthed in

South Africa, shell pendants from around 28,000 BCE were discovered in Australia, and indications of shell jewelry in Europe trace back to approximately 38,000 BCE. Intriguingly, although these cowrie shells primarily came from the Maldives, coastal regions of Africa, and the Pacific Islands, archaeological findings reveal their presence hundreds of miles inland.[1] Why would a nomadic tribe, frequently on the brink of starvation, dedicate considerable time and energy to producing or collecting fine jewelry? Furthermore, given the widespread occurrence of these cowrie shells in archaeological sites, might they have served a purpose beyond mere decoration?

Cowrie shells were used as small change in India as late as the 19th century. (1875–1876).[2]

A closer look at the inner workings of a typical nomadic band and their relations with neighboring bands is revealing. A successful hunt required a multitude of skills: Nomads needed to deeply understand the migratory patterns and instincts of the animal they were hunting, which in turn required the use of tools and tactics designed specifically for the species in question. In practice, this meant that nomadic bands typically specialized in hunting one animal: Archaeological digs in Europe show that across many sites, over 90% of the animal remains came from a single species.[3]

However, this specialization presented a significant challenge. Large herd animals, ideal for hunting, would migrate through a tribe's territory only sporadically, perhaps a few times a year. This limited the annual hunting window to a few months, raising a dilemma: While specializing in one animal was often critical for effective hunting, it posed a risk of famine during periods when that animal was absent. This precarious situation called for a solution, which was found in the form of trade. Nomadic tribes, recognizing the need to supplement their diets and resources, engaged in trade with neighboring groups who hunted different animals, thus ensuring a more stable and varied supply of food and materials.

Thankfully, each herd species followed a distinct migratory pattern, meaning that at any given time, some animals were entering a tribe's region while others were elsewhere. This ensured a continual, though varied, availability of huntable game. However, this cycle also led to a unique barter challenge. When a tribe had an abundance of meat from a successful hunt, neighboring tribes often lacked surplus resources or goods for direct exchange. One potential solution was for tribes with excess meat to lend it to those in need, with the expectation of reciprocal aid when different animals migrated into the latter's territory. Archaeological evidence, however, suggests that such joint arrangements were rare, as tribes were more inclined to engage in conflict than to establish trust-based exchanges.

Thus, just as ramen and cigarettes have emerged in modern prison systems to facilitate trade among prisoners, so too did cowry shell necklaces enable trade between tribes that were otherwise hostile. Nomads dedicated time to creating or trading for these necklaces, especially during non-hunting periods, because they knew these items held value. These necklaces, painstakingly crafted or acquired through trade, represented a medium of exchange that transcended the limitations of direct barter and the need to place trust in others. Just as language evolved to facilitate the exchange of ideas and emotions among humans, cowrie shells and other forms of early money emerged as a means of facilitating the exchange of value.

Any necklaces that were not needed for immediate trade could reliably be stored for the future, for tribes had high confidence that they would be universally accepted at a later date. This presented a marked improvement in the capacity to save for the future. While tribes had some rudimentary techniques for food preservation, the practice wasn't perfect. Preserved food was heavy to carry and still had the potential to rot; if they stowed it at a semi-permanent campsite for later use, it could be eaten by wild animals or stolen by another tribe. Thus, money unlocked a second profound use-case: the ability to preserve value and, therefore, plan for the future.

Dunbar's Number

In exploring the dynamics of ancient hunter-gatherer societies, it's noteworthy that no tribe ever expanded to a size that could support multiple sub-groups, each specializing in hunting a different herd animal. Insights from Dr. Robin Dunbar, a biological anthropologist and evolutionary psychologist, shed light on this phenomenon. In the 1990s, Dunbar explored why primates, including humans, have larger brains compared to other animals, focusing on the correlation between brain size and social capabilities. His research examined 38 primates, assessing the relationship between neocortex size (indicative of brain development) and social-group size (a measure of social complexity). Dunbar's analysis uncovered a strikingly consistent pattern: As the neocortex size increases, so does the potential size of social groups among primates. Applying this model to humans, Dunbar deduced that the human brain is capable of managing stable social relationships in groups of approximately 150 individuals, a concept now famously known as Dunbar's number. This suggests a cognitive ceiling to the number of meaningful social connections one can sustain.[4]

Reflecting on the size limitations of hunter-gatherer tribes, Dunbar's findings offer profound insights. The tribes remained small, typically not exceeding a few dozen individuals, likely because that was the upper limit of the number of trusting relationships they could cognitively manage. Humans were not neurologically equipped to form trusting bonds with a large number of individuals, a necessity for forming cooperative groups of more than ~150 people. Consequently, to expand societal cooperation beyond Dunbar's number and reach the scale of a city-state or an entire civilization, alternative strategies were required.

In this context, money emerged as a pivotal innovation, representing a tool to circumvent the cognitive limitations of trust-building in large groups. Instead of relying on trust alone, tribes could use a universally valued medium—cowrie shells—to facilitate trade and cooperation. Using a common currency thus enabled broader and more efficient exchange networks, crucial for the survival and growth of early human societies.[5]

Systems of Trust: The Company

As with money, the power of systems of trust cannot be overstated. In his seminal book *Sapiens: A Brief History of Humankind*, Professor Yuval Noah Harari explains that large-scale human cooperation was only made possible via the use of what he calls "imagined orders." According to Harari, imagined orders are shared beliefs or conceptual frameworks created by humans, allowing them to cooperate and organize at a scale beyond the limitations of Dunbar's number. At the core of every imagined order lies a solution to the fabled trust problem described previously; instead of needing to trust each other, humans can effectively cooperate by placing trust in an imagined order.[6]

If imagined orders sound confusing or abstract, it is because they are so embedded in modern society that we take them for granted. They form the very foundation of what enables us to sip an $8 latte at Starbucks, whose beans were imported from Ethiopia, served in a cup manufactured in Mexico, made from an espresso machine manufactured in Asia, and orchestrated by a company whose offices span the world and whose employees cooperate across time zones. Today, we take private enterprises like Starbucks for granted, but even the imagined order we know as "the company" did not always exist; a look back at history shows that companies were fundamental in accelerating human growth and prosperity.

Although historians dispute when companies first emerged in human history, the Dutch East India Company (or VOC), founded in 1602, is often credited as the first quasi-modern-day company. The company launched when the spice trade with the Indies was taking off. Europeans craved spices, such as cinnamon, cloves, mace, nutmeg, and pepper, but voyages were long and dangerous, rendering any spices that returned exorbitantly expensive. One voyage in

1598 began with 22 ships and returned the following year with only 12.[7]

Until the VOC was founded, an entity similar to a company that could coordinate and send continuous fleets of trading vessels to the Indies did not exist. Instead, enterprising merchants would pool their own money or desperately try to raise funds to organize a set of ships to collect spices from the Indies. If the merchants returned successfully, they would have to repeat this laborious fundraising process all over again. Two key issues related to a lack of trust emerged. First, the fundraising process for an expedition was difficult because it was hard for potential financiers to trust merchants with their funds. This largely was due to the reality of the time that any financier was held fully financially liable in the event of a failed voyage. Second, it was difficult for merchants to trust their crew because fraud and embezzlement were common occurrences during voyages.

A limited liability joint-stock company called the Dutch East India Company was thus chartered by the parliament of the Dutch Republic to solve these two separate issues of trust. Its innovative structure allowed for widespread investment, including funding from merchants, artisans, and servants, by enabling investors to purchase "shares" (what we colloquially call "stocks" today) in the company. These shares represented partial ownership in the company, allowing the investor to sell their ownership at a later time for a potential profit. In total, 1,143 people purchased shares in the VOC at inception, helping it raise around 6.5 million guilders (the Dutch currency), an immense sum at the time. Instead of needing to place their trust in individual merchants, investors in the Dutch East India Company shifted their trust to the company itself. In this collective entity, each member was incentivized to ensure its success. This setup also reduced individual financial risks, as shareholders were only liable for their investment amount, not the company's debts, a concept known as limited liability. Furthermore, compensating crew members with company shares aligned their interests with the company's success, discouraging workers from stealing or embezzling funds.[7] The innovations of limited liability and joint-stock companies together aligned incentives for all parties involved, reducing the need to trust any individual who participated in the enterprise.

The Dutch East India Company was such a success that despite the initial charter's plan to liquidate the company in 1612, the directors maintained the entity. Investors who wanted their money back had to sell their shares, inadvertently creating the world's first stock market. At first, shares were bought and sold in an open-air market. Because shares were in such high demand, a dedicated building called the *Beurs* was constructed for the purpose of stock exchange (see image below). The ambiance within the *Beurs* was rowdy, reminiscent of classic depictions of the New York Stock Exchange, with one man describing the environment on an average day: "Hand-shakes were followed by shouting, insults, impudence, pushing and shoving."[7] The innovation of the stock market further cemented the success of the company by giving potential investors the confidence they could sell their purchased shares at a moment's notice, making it easier for entrepreneurs to raise money for their budding ventures.

The Beurs, located in Amsterdam, shortly after its opening in 1611.[8]

In the following decades, the Dutch East India Company grew at an astonishing rate for the time. In the 1620s, 50 VOC ships returned from Asia with goods. In the 1690s, the number had expanded to 156. By 1760, the tonnage of shipped goods was three times that of all British shipping. The company acted as a hub for intra-Asian trade, became a major channel for Indian textile exports, and even served as the conduit for a two million guilder loan between the states of Zeeland and Holland.

The limited liability joint-stock company would serve as the institution that enabled exploration into the New World and Europe's continued global dominance. John Micklethwait and Adrian Wooldridge, authors of the book *The Company*, even claim that the creation of the company is one critical reason Europe outpaced the Middle East and China in terms of economic development.[9] However, it wasn't until the 19th century that the company gained widespread acceptance as a system of trust. Prominent figures, including economist Adam Smith, initially opposed the concept of limited liability, which at the time was a novel and unfamiliar system of trust. Initially, the formation of each company required explicit government ratification, slowing the proliferation of new companies. The railroad boom of the 19th century influenced a shift in policy, allowing companies to register without direct government approval. By the end of the 19th century, there was a surge in company creation in both the US and Europe, establishing it as the new economic standard.

At its core, the creation of the company leveraged trust in a way that had never been done before, enabling employees, investors, and entrepreneurs who did not know each other well to cooperate because the shared success of the company aligned their incentives, hence the term "corporation." As Harari described, the VOC existed nowhere but in the minds of those who owned, worked for, and recognized the company.[6] However, it was the shared trust in this imagined order that unlocked unparalleled expansion into the Indies and beyond.

Systems of Trust: Private Property Rights

The overwhelming success of the Dutch was not solely due to the rise of the limited liability joint-stock company; the Dutch Republic leveraged another system of trust—private property rights—to outcompete surrounding empires to become the world's financial center in the 17th century. The country's judicial system honored private property rights in ways that have since become the norm in developed countries today, but was unparalleled at the time compared to its European counterparts. Back then, it was only natural that European investment dollars flowed exclusively to the Dutch, where investors knew their property would be protected by the court of law and could easily be bought and sold within the newly formed stock market. Through this influx of investment dollars, Dutch merchants could raise vast sums to finance mercenary armies and massive fleets to compete with British, Portuguese, and Spanish armadas. While their country was smaller and did not command the same number of resources as other European nations, the Dutch surpassed all expectations by leveraging the power of protected property rights. As explained by investor and philanthropist Ray Dalio:

> While its small population and territorial footprint prevented it from being the dominant military power on the European continent, it more than made up for that through a combination of economic strength, financial sophistication, and a strong navy that could protect its large empire of trading posts and colonies around the world. This allowed its currency, the Dutch guilder, to emerge as the first global reserve currency.[10]

While the notion of private property is even more foundational than that of the company, the very concept of property rights did not always exist within society. Historians dispute when this concept first emerged, but it is likely that early hunter-gatherer bands lived without property rights. Many of these bands functioned as communes, where everything was shared; property belonged to the whole tribe—even relationships were rarely monogamous. It wasn't until the dawn of the Agricultural Revolution 10,000 years ago, when the majority of humanity settled into agrarian settlements, that the notion of individual property rights gained widespread adoption.

Property rights, particularly those upheld by judicial systems and recognized by government institutions, solve a crucial issue of trust vital to the functioning of advanced societies. Fundamentally, individuals are hesitant to invest in a home, start a business, or even purchase expensive goods without confidence in the security of their property. The lack of this assurance creates uncertainty over the safety of investments, leading to a significant slowdown in economic activity. In the absence of established property rights, individuals must operate in informal sectors beyond the government's reach, which diminishes the effectiveness and credibility of public institutions and further contributes to economic hardships in the country.

Today, the correlation between a country's level of development and its ability to uphold property rights is startlingly high. Hernando de Soto, a famed Peruvian economist, has spent his career researching property rights, with grim findings for those in developing countries. In Peru, de Soto tried to secure legal authorization to build a home on state-owned land; the process took nearly seven years and required dealing with 52 separate government offices. Unfortunately, such lengthy processes are not rare: In the Philippines, the process of establishing home ownership has 168 steps, involves 53 different agencies, and can last over two decades; in Haiti and Bangladesh, it can take up to 300 days to register a property. Lengthy bureaucratic processes to gain rights to build or own a home erode the effectiveness of property rights because, in practice, only the wealthy have the time and resources to navigate these processes. It is no surprise that these countries remain mired in economic distress when it is difficult, if not impossible, to put a roof over one's head. Property rights, similar to the concepts of money and corporations, form the bedrock of societal development, without which, according to de Soto,

"[You] will never be able to accomplish other reforms in a sustainable manner."[7]

With de Soto's work in mind, several truths about systems of trust emerge:

1) Systems of trust are vital to the progress of humankind because they are needed for large-scale cooperation.

2) Systems of trust are taken for granted today because they are so ingrained in our daily lives: Money, private companies, property rights, systems of law, government institutions, religions, ethical codes, etc., are all vital systems of trust.

Systems of trust emerge organically within human society because of our cognitive limitations in forming trusting relationships with many people. The ability of humans to form shared conceptual frameworks allows society to cooperate at scale without the need to trust one another directly. Money is best understood through this lens, emerging to facilitate exchange between people who did not trust each other and forming the bedrock of large-scale, global cooperation. Money also unlocks the capacity for humans to save and plan for the future in ways that previous technologies could not.

Returning to the $8 Starbucks latte mentioned earlier, to serve a single latte, hundreds of employees across dozens of companies, languages, time zones, and legal jurisdictions were likely involved. People who might not otherwise be able to communicate with each other, understand each other, or even trust each other are empowered to cooperate through the simple medium of money: An impossible exchange for food in a hunter-gatherer tribe is made trivial with the introduction of cowrie shell money. Those who have traveled to a foreign country without a shared common language know this well. Although verbal communication may be challenging or even unfeasible, the use of money provides a universal language for negotiating the price of goods, making the process of purchasing items remarkably straightforward.

Trust-based systems are deeply embedded in our everyday lives. As such, they are often taken for granted, with many overlooking their crucial role in human prosperity. This is particularly true for money, which is sometimes mistakenly labeled as "inherently evil" due to a failure to recognize its role in addressing fundamental human needs. It is not money itself, but rather flaws in creating and managing monetary systems that lead to societal inequalities and challenges—topics this book will explore in later chapters. Money is best understood as a technology, arguably the most potent trust mechanism created by humans, as it facilitates economic interaction and exchange between individuals globally. In the words of Harari, "Money is the most universal and most efficient system of mutual trust ever devised."[6] The next chapter of this book will explore money's role as a technology throughout history, drawing insights from its past successes and failures to build an understanding of the properties of the technology itself.

CHAPTER 2

THE ASCENT OF MONEY

On January 24, 1848, James Wilson Marshall made a momentous discovery on the banks of the American River near Coloma, California, at the foot of the Sierra Nevada mountain range. He spotted a gleaming metallic object in the river's waters, immediately identifying it as gold. Marshall was in the area under the employment of John Sutter to construct a sawmill, but with this discovery, they quickly diverted their efforts to panning for gold. Despite attempts to keep the finding a secret, by mid-March, a local newspaper reported that vast amounts of gold had been found near Sutter's sawmill. Marshall's discovery would rapidly transform the economy of the Californian colony, ushering in an era known today as the gold rush.

At the time of his discovery, California was sparsely populated, occupied by roughly 150,000 Native Americans, 6,500 Californios (people of Spanish or Mexican descent), and 700 foreigners. These numbers quickly multiplied as people received word of the abundance of gold in the Sierra Nevada region. Within months of the discovery, trappers from Oregon, Mormons from Utah, miners from Mexico and Chile, sailors from Hawaii, and farmers from the Chinese province of Kwangtung all came pouring into the area.[1] An onslaught of Americans from the East Coast began in December 1848 after President James Polk announced, "The accounts of abundance of gold are of such an extraordinary character as would scarcely command belief were they not corroborated by the authentic reports of officers in the public service."[2] By the end of 1848, the non-native population of California had grown from 700 to 20,000; by the end of 1849, that number again multiplied five-fold.[2]

An 1849 handbill advertising transit to the "gold regions."[3]

San Francisco, then a nearby port town, saw a drastic reduction in its male population as many rushed to the Sierra Nevada in search of gold. Men lured by the promise of gold from across the United States took significant physical and financial risks, including taking on large amounts of debt, spending their life savings, or selling their homes to journey to California. The sudden influx of people led to the rapid expansion of mining towns, which were often plagued by lawlessness, including rampant gambling, alcoholism, prostitution, and violence. All of this was not in vain, however, with the gold rush producing a staggering amount of gold: $10 million in 1849, $41 million in 1850, and many multiples more in the following years.[4] Altogether, several billion dollars' worth of gold (in today's dollars) were mined in just several years, ushering in one of the most influential American events before 1850.

Why do humans have a universal infatuation with gold, to such an extent that *the mere prospect* of it was enough to convince thousands of Americans to uproot their lives and face death crossing the Great Plains and mountain states? The answer was simple: At the time, gold was widely viewed as money, serving as the backing of many national currencies. This universal acceptance of gold's value formed the kindling that fueled the gold rush bonfire.

Gold had served this role for thousands of years, first emerging as money within the Lydian Empire in the 6th century BCE. Independently, many other civilizations adopted gold as money around the same period, including the Greeks, the Aztecs, the Chinese, and societies throughout the Middle East.[5,6,7,8]

What made gold the preeminent and universal choice of money by the 19th century over countless alternatives such as silver, bronze, and cowrie shells? Exploring this question unveils surprising truths about the nature of money, offering insights into the development of our modern monetary system. This evolution is not just a financial transformation, but also a reflection of the advancement of human society at large.

Cowrie Shells

Let us return to the nomadic tribes of 38,000 BCE, who formed small bands that typically specialized in hunting a single herding animal. Interactions between these bands brought one of two outcomes: armed conflict or the trade of goods priced in cowrie shells. Why were cowrie shells commonly used as the accepted currency rather than any other everyday item at the time, such as nuts, clothing, or precious stones?

The nomadic lifestyle of these hunter-gatherers meant they were in constant search of the next patch of tuber vegetables or huntable animals. While these nomads typically remained within a swath of land they protected as their territory, they rarely settled in a particular area for more than a few days. This lifestyle demanded carrying nearly all possessions on their backs, only occasionally storing valuables or tools such as clay pots in frequently visited campsites. Anything one wanted to keep more permanently would be carried, including collectibles used as money.

Naturally, any form of money used for trade needed to be portable enough to fit into a small pack or pocket and durable enough to withstand rugged travel conditions. These requirements ruled out perishable foodstuffs, bulky precious stones, and space-consuming spare clothing.

When conducting trade, hunter-gatherers needed to use items that were widely accepted by neighboring tribes and were "divisible" or small enough to use for the purchase of goods that varied widely in price. While rare gems were durable enough to warrant carrying for many months, they were too valuable for the daily trade of food and garments.

Cowrie shell necklaces conveniently satisfied many of these requirements, making them fit to serve as money. They were lightweight enough to be worn around the neck or wrist, durable enough to last indefinitely, and could easily be combined or divided to accommodate trade for goods of varying value. Their intrinsic aesthetic appeal added to their acceptability across tribes with varying customs, beliefs, and languages, making them a practical and versatile form of currency in the prehistoric hunter-gatherer economy.

Perhaps the most valuable quality of cowrie shells was their inherent scarcity, a result of natural rarity coupled with the time required to manufacture beautiful necklaces. Cowrie shells couldn't be counterfeited by hunter-gatherers, giving recipients confidence that they were legitimately harvested from the coastline. Hours of labor were needed to improve the aesthetics of a shell collected from a beach into one worthy of adornment. Thus, those selling valuable foodstuffs for cowrie shell necklaces had the confidence that the necklaces would retain their value over a long period.

Ultimately, the advent of global trade brought the demise of cowrie shells' role as money. Low-cost shipping routes opened between the Maldives, where the shells were harvested, and the rest of the world. The net effect was a drop in the scarcity of cowrie shells, as they now flooded into areas where they were once highly valued. Over time, this inflation caused holders of cowrie shells to lose trust that the shells would hold their value over a long period.[5] Thus, cowrie shells were no longer an effective system of trust for coordinating trade because they could not be trusted as a reliable medium of exchange or store of value. Such is the evolution of money throughout human history: Scarcity plays a fundamental role in the rise and fall of currencies. Commodity* goods with natural scarcity tend to be adopted by civilizations as currency and lose their currency status when an external force, such as the development of new technology, changes their natural scarcity.

Wampum

Native Americans faced a similar issue with the arrival of colonists in the New World. These tribes had been using strings of white and bluish-black clamshell beads called wampum for millennia as a commonly accepted currency, with some of them, such as the Narragansetts

---

* Commodities are basic raw materials and goods used to manufacture products. Examples include oil, wheat, and gold.

of modern-day Rhode Island, specializing in its manufacture. While wampum originated from the East Coast, its use spread far inland, with tribes such as the Iroquois, who lived more than a hundred miles from the shore in modern-day New York, amassing large sums of it from tribute.[9]

When colonists arrived in the New World, they lacked a formal currency. At the time, the British Crown forbade the use of gold and silver coins in its colonies, as this would have risked the outflow of these metals from Britain. Such a policy aimed to maintain colonial dependency on Britain, as the lack of a common, stable currency helped prevent the growth of independent trade between colonies. While initially hesitant, colonists eventually adopted wampum as currency through frequent interaction and trade with local Native American tribes. It gained such widespread adoption that New England recognized it as legal tender in 1637, meaning colonists could pay their taxes with wampum. The Dutch governor of New Amsterdam even took out a sizable loan in wampum, and colonists began to refer to money using the word "clam."[5]

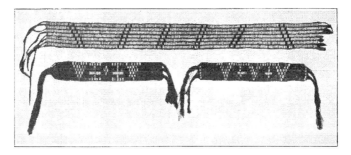

Necklace of wampum.[10]

The use of wampum as an official form of currency changed when profit-seeking colonists began using steel drills to manufacture wampum beads en masse. What once required skilled laborers much time to craft could now be made by an unskilled laborer in a small fraction of the time. The market was soon flooded with wampum beads, ruining the natural scarcity that Native American tribes had enjoyed for millennia. Tribes like the Narragansetts, who once prided themselves on the manufacture of wampum necklaces, had to resort to other means of work, as wampum lost nearly all of its value save its use as ornamental jewelry.[5]

Similar to cowrie shells, wampum functioned as the region's currency for thousands of years before the arrival of Europeans because it carried a set of properties that made it ideal for trade: Wampum was small and portable, its component clam shells were durable, the beads were small enough to facilitate even the smallest of trades, its aesthetic quality made it widely acceptable by tribes across America, and the clams were sufficiently scarce to give natives confidence that wampum could retain value over time. These qualities allowed indigenous tribes to place considerable trust in the value of wampum as money. It was only with the introduction of new technology—the steel drill—that its natural scarcity changed. This change eroded the trust in wampum's effectiveness built over time, ruining its monetary value and causing those in the New World to turn to other commodities for currency.

Tobacco

While wampum gained widespread monetary adoption in New England in the first half of the 17th century, tobacco became the widely accepted currency of the American South. At its peak, tobacco was considered legal tender in Virginia, Maryland, and North Carolina. Like wampum, it was highly divisible, durable when adequately dried, lightweight enough to be portable, and was widely accepted across the South as a currency due to its intrinsic value. In contrast to wampum and cowrie shells, however, tobacco did not have the same natural scarcity. Once decreed as legal tender, its value rose tremendously, leading farmers to grow as much as they possibly could. As a result, the economy was flooded with new tobacco, destroying its scarcity—and, therefore, its value.

In an effort to uphold tobacco as a viable currency, colonial governments restricted tobacco production to farmers who received official authorization. Not only was this policy unfair, but it also failed to solve the root cause of the issue. Farmers granted authorization could grow as much tobacco as they wanted, for there was no natural limit as there was with wampum and cowrie shells.

Tobacco also proved to be a cumbersome currency because it lacked uniformity. Unlike dollar bills, which are identical, no two pounds of tobacco are the same. Tobacco has a wide range of varieties and qualities, leading to a host of complications. The subjectivity of tobacco quality rendered trade more difficult, as traders would inevitably come to disagreements over the quality of tobacco being exchanged. Furthermore, because tobacco was recognized as legal tender, farmers were incentivized to use the lowest quality tobacco to pay taxes and purchase goods, with full faith that it would be accepted as currency. All high-quality tobacco grown was saved and sold to Europeans, leading to a slow decline in the quality of tobacco used as currency.[8]

Eventually, a "tobacco standard" was created to solve the quality problem. A centralized rating authority was created to assess the quality of tobacco, which was packaged and stored in a series of public warehouses. Standardized bills, backed by the stored tobacco, were issued, creating a system remarkably similar to the gold standard later implemented in the US, where US dollar bills were backed by gold stored in government vaults. This system held the confidence of Virginian citizens because they knew that at any time, they could redeem their bills for the stored tobacco that backed the bill. These "tobacco notes," as they came to be known, gained official legal tender status in Virginia by 1727 and would remain in use for the rest of the 18th century.

Path Dependence and Evolution

The stories of cowrie shells, wampum, and tobacco shed light on the emergence and progression of money within society. Money's rise within prehistoric and pre-industrial societies was not random, nor was its progression haphazard. Instead, money evolved organically, with societies initially adopting various commodities as proto-monies, gradually converging over time on those that most effectively served monetary functions, namely to trade and preserve wealth. The choice of currency in any society at a given time was influenced by the political decisions that constrained what could be used and the practical availability of commodities suitable for use as money. This phenomenon, known as path dependence, is crucial for understanding the current role and form of money in society.

Path dependence is the idea that the present state of a technology or system results from the cumulative impact of historical, pragmatic decisions made along the path of its development. These decisions, often based on the context and knowledge available at the time, set a course for a technology that becomes increasingly difficult to alter as it evolves and the layers of investment, habitual use, and infrastructure built upon it. A common example is today's QWERTY keyboard. The layout of the keys harkens back to the 19th century when typewriters served as the writing tool of choice. Typewriters commonly jammed when adjacent keys were pressed in quick succession, necessitating a redesign of the key layout. The QWERTY layout design that we use today is a result of the need to arrange keys in such a way as to minimize the jamming of mechanical typewriters as opposed to prioritizing typing speed. This layout remains with us to this day because up-and-coming computer companies have no reason to change the keyboard layout for marginal improvements in typing speed at the risk of alienating customers accustomed to the typewriter's QWERTY layout. Therefore, today's computer keyboards are path-dependent on the historical decisions motivating the original and continued use of the QWERTY keyboard layout.

Early monies emerged in a similar fashion. The hunter-gatherer societies of times gone by almost certainly never held a meeting discussing the need for a currency to help them facilitate trade with neighboring tribes; rather, their cowrie shell necklaces already had an intrinsic value* based on their cultural significance and aesthetic appeal, making them the most practical option available for intermediating trade. In parts of Africa, these shells lasted well into the 20th century as accepted money, not because they were the most suitable money of the time, but because the path dependence of their adoption cemented their long-lasting monetary and cultural value.

Likewise, in the early period of the American colonies, colonists resorted to using tobacco or

---

* A quality or property of a good that has value, independent of its market price. Gold's intrinsic value comes from a combination of its beautiful aesthetic and metallurgic properties that make it a good choice for building electronics.

wampum, not because they were ideal forms of money, but because of their immediate availability and practicality. The British Crown's prohibition on the use of metallic coins in the colonies played a significant role in this choice. Consequently, the colonies adapted by using the most accessible commodities at hand: wampum in New England and tobacco in Virginia. The combination of political decision-making from the British, alongside what was pragmatically available as a commodity, ultimately determined the colonies' original currency systems. Later in this book, we will explore how contemporary monetary systems can similarly be understood through the concept of path dependence.

In 1715, colonial currencies were varied, with legal tender status given to 17 different commodities, including wampum, tobacco, wheat, maize, and other foodstuffs. This was purely the result of the colonies' lack of a single authority to impose a common currency. Thus, each colony needed to resort to using any medium that could easily support trade and the preservation of wealth. These currencies slowly faded as the colonies coalesced around using fewer options, with the principles of Darwinian evolution dictating the survival of the fittest currency.

The British evolutionary biologist Richard Dawkins of the University of Oxford popularized the application of evolution to systems outside of the biological world. In his book *The Selfish Gene*, Dawkins expands upon the work of Charles Darwin, offering several key updates and insights about Darwin's theory of evolution. One of his most intriguing concepts is the notion that evolutionary mechanisms govern how ideas proliferate and evolve within a culture and, more broadly, across civilizations. Echoing Darwin's theory that genes mutate randomly, with the most advantageous mutations being passed down through generations, Dawkins suggests that ideas within a society undergo a similar process. As ideas are shared among individuals, they "mutate," and those with the greatest cultural resonance spread most effectively, essentially "surviving as the fittest" in a vast pool of competing concepts. Dawkins coined the term "memes" to describe ideas that spread person-to-person within a society—a term which today fittingly applies to viral internet content.[11]

Dawkins' application of evolutionary principles extends beyond the realm of ideas to encompass the development and proliferation of technologies in society, including money. Scottish historian Niall Ferguson succinctly captures this idea, stating,

"Financial history is essentially the result of institutional mutation and natural selection."[5] This phenomenon is illustrated in colonial America, where an initial diversity of 17 different currencies gradually narrowed down to two—gold and silver—as they outperformed other available choices. The consolidation of currency was formalized after the Revolutionary War with the passage of the Coinage Act of 1792, when the United States established its mint and declared a bimetallic dollar standard as the national currency consisting of gold and silver coins. It wasn't until after the Civil War that the US dropped silver coinage in 1873, moving to a de facto gold-based system that marked the apex of money's evolution in the pre-industrial era.* This period, known as the Gilded Age, spanned the latter half of the 19th century and was marked by peace, stability, and significant economic growth.

Great Britain had been much quicker to adopt gold, implementing a gold standard in 1717. Under this system, gold reserves held by Great Britain's central bank underpinned the paper currency issued to the

---

* It was not until the Gold Standard Act of 1900 that the United States definitively adopted the gold standard. This act confirmed that gold was the only standard for redeeming paper money, effectively ending bimetallism.[12]

public. This system was initially created under the guidance of Sir Isaac Newton, who served as warden of the Royal Mint. The British gold standard was adopted across the far reaches of the British Empire, significantly streamlining its international trade by eliminating the need for merchants to use multiple currencies along their trading routes. Following the Franco-Prussian War in 1871, other major European powers adopted gold standards, ushering in a period of prosperity known as La Belle Époque. By 1900, all industrialized nations had officially adopted the gold standard, which lasted across Europe until the onset of World War I in 1914.

Why did gold outperform all other options to become the globally accepted "fittest" money by the end of the 19th century? Reflecting on the successes and failures of cowrie shells, wampum, and tobacco, seven properties emerge that dictate the suitability of a commodity to serve as money and explain why pre-industrial societies converged on using gold as the fittest form of money:

Portability

Portability is the ease with which money can be transported for trade or storage. The hunter-gatherer societies that used cowrie shells exemplified the importance of portability, as they needed to carry nearly all lively possessions with them day-to-day. Any item or commodity too cumbersome to transport on a daily basis would not have worked as a currency for the hunter-gatherers.

Because gold is both rare and dense, it proved to be more portable than most alternatives. Even small amounts of gold held substantial value, making it easy for merchants, traders, and anyone covering significant distances to carry considerable wealth without taking up much space.

Durability

Durability is the ability of money to withstand physical degradation over long periods. Shells, as used in cowrie necklaces and wampum, were excellent forms of early money because they were one of the most durable options available to prehistoric societies. Larger shells rarely broke, even in the roughest of travel conditions.

Despite the robustness of shells, gold is markedly more durable. Due to its metallurgic properties, gold cannot rust nor corrode, qualities that copper and silver cannot claim, enabling gold to retain its integrity over indefinite periods.

Divisibility

Divisibility is the degree to which money can be divided into small units to facilitate trade for low-value items. Wampum exemplified divisibility, as Native Americans would take apart necklaces to trade small quantities of beads when trading for minor items.

Given that gold can easily be melted down into small coins of various sizes and denominations, it can be transformed into units small enough for the needs of its users. Issuers of gold coins had flexibility in the denominations and, thus, the divisibility of the gold coins they could create, whereas issuers of wampum were constrained by the sizes of clams they could collect.

Many countries, including the United States, at multiple times throughout its history, issued silver coins alongside gold coins precisely because they were more divisible. With silver being valued significantly lower than gold, it was used for small-value purchases in a similar way that change is used today.

Acceptability

Acceptability is the degree to which money is universally recognized across society. Early monies emerged in part due to their intrinsic value. An item with intrinsic value, such as tobacco, by definition, is already widely used and, thus, is more readily accepted by society as currency. Wampum and cowrie shells became universally acceptable because they already had cultural and aesthetic intrinsic value, making it easy to convince a neighboring tribe to accept wampum as payment for a proposed trade.

Gold proved to be superior to every alternative in terms of acceptability due to its universal appeal across recorded history.

Verifiability

Verifiability is the ability to authenticate if money is real or counterfeit. In the era preceding industrialization, items such as cowrie shell necklaces and wampum boasted high levels of verifiability. In the absence of methods to fabricate counterfeit shell necklaces, their authenticity could be easily determined through mere observation. Conversely, tobacco's verifiability was limited due to the subjective nature of assessing its quality, which often couldn't be definitively judged without actually using the tobacco.

Gold coins represented a significant advancement in verifiability compared to their predecessors. Embossing each coin with a distinctive insignia, a mark of the issuing government authority, facilitated the process of user validation. This stamp not only assured users of the coin's legitimacy but also erected a formidable barrier against the production of convincing forgeries. However, gold coins do not have perfect verifiability, as forgers occasionally can craft coins with markings that closely mimic the official governmental insignia.

Notably, inhabitants of Ancient Rome developed a unique method to confirm the authenticity of their coins. During the later years of the Roman Empire, emperors clandestinely diluted their currency by incorporating other metals (a process known as debasement). These coins maintained the appearance of being made of gold and silver, enabling the emperors to produce more coins than would be possible with pure gold and silver alone. Roman citizens devised a technique to assess a coin's purity: Striking it against a hard surface would produce a melodic ring if the coin was pure, but a dull sound if it was impure. Consequently, the term "sound" came to be associated with pure coins and has endured to this day to denote stable and trustworthy currency (i.e., "sound" money).

Uniformity

Uniformity is the consistency between different units of money issued. Tobacco demonstrates the importance of uniformity: Because tobacco leaves have a wide range of qualities, it was difficult for traders to assess the exact value of a pound of tobacco when trading, ultimately necessitating the elaborate creation of a "tobacco standard" in an attempt to bring uniformity to the currency. Monies that are more uniform are easier to transact with.

Minted gold coins are identical to one another, serving as an improvement over previous commodity monies such as wampum or tobacco that had significant variances in uniformity.

Scarcity

Perhaps the most important of the seven properties, scarcity, defines how easily money may be produced or expanded in supply. Humans have always gone to great lengths to produce money however possible. Tobacco proved how easily producible money can be abused. Wampum and cowrie shells demonstrated that currencies with natural scarcity perform well. However, technological developments can irreversibly reduce the scarcity of money, thereby ruining its value.

The most significant attribute of gold is its scarcity in the Earth's crust. Because of its rarity, gold supply does not spike, even when companies pour large sums of money into its mining. As a result, historically, the annual increase in gold supply rarely exceeds 2%. Even notable surges such as the California gold rush did not meaningfully impact gold's relative scarcity over other commodities. This inherent scarcity has been a key driver of gold's historical role as money and continues to be the primary reason why some still support its use as a monetary standard today.

With these properties in mind, it becomes evident that money is not merely any item society accepts and trusts as a medium of exchange, as it is often defined. Instead, money is more accurately described as a technology that embodies these seven properties that in turn help it gain societal adoption and trust. In the chart below, when comparing gold with other historical forms of money, it is clear how gold is superior when assessed from the perspective of money's seven properties. Historically, forms of money that have failed typically did so because they lacked one or more of these seven essential properties. For instance, tobacco, wampum, and cowrie shells all fell out of favor as a result of their respective losses in scarcity and other deficiencies.

The Pre-Industrial Properties of Money

	Portability	Durability	Divisibility	Acceptability	Verifiability	Uniformity	Scarcity
Cowrie Shell	×	×	×	×	×		
Wampum	×	×	×	×	×		
Tobacco	×	×	×	×			
Gold	×	×	×	×	×	×	×

Ultimately, gold gained prominence through a process of evolution, out-competing all other existing monies to become the premier money of pre-industrial societies, precisely because it best satisfied these seven properties. It was not by mere chance, or simply because gold is aesthetically appealing to the eye, that it gained prominence within the ancient Sumerian, Lydian, Egyptian, Greek, Roman, Byzantine, and Chinese dynasties; it did so because money is a technology vital to the flourishing of human civilization and gold was the best commodity equipped to satisfy this function.

As seen in Chapter 1, money arose from the need to coordinate trade between two parties that did not trust each other. In facilitating trade, money helped hunter-gatherer tribes specialize in hunting a single animal with the assurance that when food was scarce, they could trade cowrie shells for much-needed sustenance. Money also empowered these tribes to save for the future. In times of abundance, they traded excess food for cowrie shell necklaces from other tribes, a currency they knew could be used at a later point to trade for food when their supplies ran out.

Today, money's functions as a medium of exchange and a store of value remain essential, yet at a much larger scale. Therefore, when the money adopted by society adheres to these seven properties, it empowers society to save for the future and facilitates increased domestic and international trade, two fundamental components to a well-functioning economy and flourishing society. The Gilded Age in the United States and La Belle Époque in Europe in the latter half of the 19th century serve as excellent examples of what the world looks like when it collectively utilizes the optimal form of money. As described by the Federal Reserve Bank of St. Louis:

> The period from 1880 to 1914, known as the heyday of the gold standard, was a remarkable period in world economic history. It was characterized by rapid economic growth, the free flow of labor and capital across political borders, virtually free trade and, in general, world peace.[13]

However, this period of sustained growth and widespread prosperity under the gold standard was short-lived. The turn of the century brought a series of technological innovations that would fundamentally reduce the effectiveness of gold as global money. With the world entering its first global conflict in 1914, the fate of gold was sealed, leading to its eventual replacement with a new form of money that would shape the course of history throughout the 20th century.

PART II

MONEY OF THE PRESENT

CHAPTER 3

GOLD, BLOOD, AND POWER

"What hath God wrought!" were the famous four words of the first telegraph transmission sent on May 24, 1844. The telegraph had been many years in the making, with a creation story as fascinating as its impact on the world would be profound. Its invention was credited to an unexpected man, Samuel J. Morse, who began his career as a painter, eventually becoming a professor of painting and sculpture at the University of the City of New York. While working overseas on a commissioned art project, Morse received word of his wife's death. Unfortunately, due to the limitations of the era's communication methods, which relied on ship transit, he received this news only after her burial. This delay sparked a realization in Morse: There was a great need for a faster means of transmitting news, one that could outpace the speed of ships.

While on a return voyage to the United States, Morse overheard a conversation between two gentlemen discussing a recent invention by Michael

Faraday: the electromagnet. It occurred to Morse that such a device could be used to transmit encoded messages over a wire. Upon his return to the US, Morse elicited the help of Leonard Gale, a fellow scholar who taught chemistry. Between Gale's knowledge of modern electrical technology and Morse's clever invention of an encoding language that would come to be known as the Morse code, the two of them built a working "telegraph" system within a few years.

In 1843, Morse submitted a proposal to the US government, which was then offering a $30,000 prize for a viable plan to establish a communication system along the Atlantic coast. Following his submission, Congress approved funding for Morse to build a telegraph line between Baltimore and Washington, DC, as a pilot for his concept. The initial plan involved laying pipes to run the wires underground between the two cities. However, the project had its challenges. Defective materials, coupled with a strict project timeline, led to a change in approach: Wires were hastily strung overhead using trees and poles. This practical solution inadvertently established the standard for overhead telegraph lines.

Morse's successful transmission marked the beginning of the global spread of the telegraph. By 1851, the United States alone boasted 50 telegraph companies. A decade later, in 1861, the completion of the first transcontinental telegraph line connected San Francisco with the East Coast. This expansion continued rapidly, and by 1866, the first transatlantic cables were laid, further bridging global communication.[1,2,3]

The telegraph's rapid expansion in the late 19th century significantly impacted the global monetary system. Before telecommunications, the speed of physical transit limited domestic and international financial transactions, as gold needed to be manually transported by foot, horse, or ship to settle trades. The advent of the telegraph transformed this process, enabling almost instantaneous international monetary transactions. This innovation paved the way for the development of global banking systems, which facilitated new types of transactions communicated via telegraph.

With this technological breakthrough, banks could now "net" multiple transactions instead of settling each trade with a direct exchange of money for goods. For example, if Person A sold apples to Person B for $10, and Person B sold $5 worth of bananas and $6 worth of oranges to Person A, the banks could simply conduct a single transaction. In this case, they would transfer $1 from Person B's account to Person A's, representing the "net" total of money movement between the two parties. This streamlined approach to banking and trade significantly increased the efficiency and speed of financial transactions worldwide.

The results of these innovations were twofold: Now that transactions could be conducted nearly instantaneously, speed, for the first time, became an important property of money (see the chart below on money's updated properties). While the scarcity and durability of gold still made it an excellent store of value, its function as a medium of exchange did not live up to the speed now needed in money. Secondly, because banks could now net transactions across their accounts, there was a much smaller need for physical gold, as ledgers could now be accurately maintained to track money movement between different bank institutions. This, in turn, incentivized the centralization of the banking industry, as larger banks that could coordinate substantial volumes of transactions were more efficient than smaller banks that handled low transaction volumes.[4]

An emerging trend became evident: Gold, traditionally circulating as coins throughout the economy, would be predominantly stored in the secure vaults of banks and savings institutions. In place of physical gold coins, paper certificates came to the fore, which were issued by banks and redeemable for gold upon request. This shift to paper money presented clear advantages in an evolving economic landscape. It allowed for wealth to be transferred and secured more swiftly and reliably, meeting the demands of an increasingly interconnected and fast-paced economy.*

---

* Beyond the scope of this book is the concept of fractional reserve banking, a system where banks hold only a fraction of their depositors' money in reserve, lending out the remainder to earn interest and create new money. The emergence of paper money allowed banks to begin fractional reserve lending practices for the first time. Interested readers are advised to read further about the role played by fractional reserve banking in our past and present financial systems.

An Update to the Properties of Money Following the Invention of the Telegraph

	Portability	Durability	Divisibility	Acceptability	Verifiability	Uniformity	Scarcity	Speed
Cowrie Shell	×	×	×	×	×			
Wampum	×	×	×	×	×			
Tobacco	×	×	×	×				
Gold	×	×	×	×	×	×	×	
Gold Backed Paper Currency	×	×	×	×	×	×	×	×

The success of paper money certificates hinged on trust in intermediaries responsible for safeguarding the gold reserves. Initially, these intermediaries, primarily private banks, each issued their distinct forms of paper money, commonly referred to as banknotes. This practice led to a cluttered and often confusing financial landscape, especially in regions with many competing intermediary banks, each with its own type of banknote. The situation led to a pressing need for a more uniform and standardized paper currency. This need for standardization and its implications are further explored in Columbia Business School Professor Omid Malekan's book *Re-Architecting Trust*:

> The proliferation of privately issued paper money created the need for a new type of standardization. The more banknotes gained traction in an economy, the harder it was to keep track of which receipts were backed by which coins held by which bank. This problem was particularly acute in regions where neighboring cities each had their own coins, banks, and paper money. The multitudes of money and institutions made it more cumbersome to verify authenticity and easier to pass counterfeits. Like the metal money that came before it, paper money was

in dire need of standardization. Since most governments already maintained a monopoly on coin issuance, and the original point of paper money was to create a more convenient way to transfer ownership of metal, it made sense for the same governments that issued the coins to also issue the paper.[5]

In the United States, the diverse range of privately issued paper certificates eventually consolidated into standardized paper money issued by the US Treasury. This uniformity in government-issued currency facilitated seamless commerce across states. The federal government's commitment to exchange these bills for gold at a fixed rate is what underpinned trust in this evolving monetary system.

$10,000 1882 Gold Certificate.[6]

However, the US government eventually faced scenarios that necessitated spending beyond its means, particularly during times of military conflict. In these instances, devaluing the dollar's exchange rate to gold or suspending the dollar's convertibility into gold altogether proved to be a more suitable method of raising funds than increasing taxes. For example, suppose the United States sets the value of one ounce of gold at $5, meaning any US citizen can "redeem" $5 with the government in exchange for an ounce of gold. Later, the government updates this exchange rate, setting it to $10 per ounce of gold. Now, each dollar is devalued, worth 0.1 ounces of gold instead of 0.2 ounces. The government prints an additional $5 of paper bills per ounce of gold in its reserves to support this new exchange rate, granting themselves additional money to finance expenditures. This same process of currency devaluation also occurred among other great powers on a global scale. Consequently, paper currency, originally introduced to simplify trade, increasingly became a tool wielded by governments for financing wars and other significant expenditures such as World War I.

At the onset of World War I in the summer of 1914, a widespread belief prevailed that the conflict would be brief. Kaiser Wilhelm II famously assured his troops, "You will be home before the leaves have fallen from the trees."[7] This expectation was rooted in the historical precedent of short-lived wars, often constrained by the limited resources of the belligerents. However, World War I marked a profound transformation in military conflict. Armies were now heavily industrialized, armed with machine guns, chemical weapons, and nascent forms of tanks. Perhaps most importantly, governments wielded a novel and powerful tool that could extend the length of wars indefinitely: the ability to print money.

As 1914 drew to a close, it became evident that the war would defy expectations of brevity. Initially, Germany, France, and Britain had managed to fund their war efforts by liquidating gold reserves. Germany's stockpile, amounting to £70 million, was significant for the era.[8] When the future British Prime Minister Lloyd George was reminded of Germany's substantial gold reserves on the war's eve, he remarked, "A mighty sum, but England will raise the last million."[8] This statement would prove remarkably prophetic.

By November 1914, the warring nations turned to extensive borrowing to sustain their military expenditures. That month, the British government turned to the public to raise funds for the war by issuing bonds. These bonds were a form of debt that the government promised to repay with interest at a later date. On November 23, 1914, just after Britain's first war bond issuance, the *Financial Times of London* optimistically reported that the war bonds were "oversubscribed," suggesting an enthusiastic public response and a robust financial position for Britain. This coverage implied overwhelming public support for the war effort, which reportedly "offered the Government every penny it asked for—and more."[9]

The public was thus led to believe that support for the war was overwhelming. In reality, the supposed success of the issuance was a facade: Britain's initial attempt to raise war bonds was significantly undersubscribed, meaning that the government was unable to sell as many bonds as it had hoped—in fact, less than a third of its original target.[9] Had this news been made public, the under-subscription would have indicated a lack of public confidence or available capital among the population to invest in these bonds. To avoid publicizing this failure, the Bank of England intervened clandestinely. It printed new money and secretly channeled it through its chief cashier and his deputy, who then used these funds to buy bonds under their own names. This covert action effectively masked the shortfall in the bond issue.[10] John Maynard Keynes, a prominent 20th-century British economist aware of this deception, lauded the government's actions as "masterly manipulation."[9] The truth of this financial maneuvering only became public knowledge a century later through a 2017 memo released by Bank of England researchers and a subsequent correction by *The Times*.[11]

However, the public was not privy to this information at the time. After this successful manipulation by the British government, the precedent was set to continue issuing war bonds. Across Europe, national debts surged dramatically. Britain's national debt grew more than tenfold between 1914 and 1919. France saw its debt as a percentage of gross domestic product* escalate from 66% to 170%. Germany, having already depleted its gold reserves, witnessed its debt balloon from five billion marks in 1914 to 156 billion by 1918.[8]

Despite substantial loans from the United States to its European allies, the debt incurred by the warring nations simply exceeded the lending capacity available to them. Taxes had been raised to historic levels and could no longer be used to increase government revenues. Consequently, for countries like Germany, France, and Britain, the remaining viable strategy to

---

* Gross domestic product, or GDP, is a commonly used measure of the size of an economy, representing the total output of a country's economy in one year.

sustain their war efforts was the issuance of additional currency, essentially printing money.*

This practice of generating currency "out of thin air" theoretically offered these nations an indefinite means of financing their war endeavors. However, this approach came with a significant economic trade-off, particularly concerning the stability and integrity of the currency. The core issue revolved around the concept of gold redeemability. In a gold standard monetary system, where the volume of paper currency increases while the gold reserves underpinning this currency remain unchanged, a fundamental imbalance develops. This discrepancy threatens the currency's value; as the supply of paper money surges, each unit's proportionate backing in gold diminishes.

---

* In most cases, a given nation's money creation is carried out by their central bank. Throughout this book, central banks and governments will often be referred to as the same entity. Most central banks, including the Federal Reserve, are technically "independent" from the government as institutions that are neither public nor private. In reality, because central banks are legally owned by the government, operate in coordination with them, and are run by government-appointed members, they are best thought of as an extension of the government. Therefore, when the phrase "governments print money" is used, it is a simplification of the true method used to print money involving central banks, with the same net outcome.

Therefore, in the name of national security, the gold standard was abandoned across Europe. With the exception of the US, every nation engaged in World War I abandoned the gold standard in 1914.[12] This departure meant their currencies were no longer anchored to concrete assets, enabling these countries to freely print currency to sustain their war expenditures. By leaving the gold standard, European nations began using "fiat currency"—a type of money that has no physical backing and derives its value entirely from trust in the governing state, which maintains complete control over its supply.

At this moment, money's path dependence was at direct odds with its evolutionary development: The short-term necessity to win the war trumped the demand to maintain a hard, scarce currency. Thus, in general, for money to maintain scarcity over time, it must be incorruptible to the immediate needs of the government issuing it. This idea will be explored in more detail later in this book in the context of modern-day money.

Properties of Money - Updated with the Emergence of Fiat Money in WWI

	Portability	Durability	Divisibility	Acceptability	Verifiability	Uniformity	Scarcity	Speed
Cowrie Shell	×	×	×	×				
Wampum	×	×	×	×	×			
Tobacco	×	×	×	×				
Gold	×	×	×	×	×	×	×	
Gold Backed Paper Currency	×	×	×	×	×	×	×	×
Fiat Currency	×	×	×	×	×	×		×

With regard to this abandonment of the gold standard, famed Austrian economist Ludwig von Mises said in a 1960 lecture:

> Governments believe that when there is a choice between an unpopular tax and a very popular expenditure, there is a way out for them—the way toward inflation. This illustrates the problem of going away from the gold standard.[13]

As a result of immense government spending and requisite money creation during World War I, Europeans suffered crippling levels of inflation in the late 1910s that eroded trust in their institutions. This distrust further complicated government borrowing efforts, causing an even greater reliance on money printing.

Germany serves as a notable example of this phenomenon. Post war, the Allied powers demanded substantial reparations from the defeated Germany, as stipulated in the Treaty of Versailles. Similar to the costs of the war, these reparations exceeded what could be reasonably financed through taxation alone. Consequently, Germany resorted to printing its currency, the mark, at an astonishing rate. The inflation rate was so severe that the mark's exchange rate to the US dollar skyrocketed from 57 in 1921 to 5.7 *billion* by 1923. To illustrate, this is akin to the price of a Big Mac rising from $5 today to $500 million in just two years. Behold the power of money printing.

A 500 billion mark banknote from Weimar Germany, 1923.[14]

The story of World War I offers a few lessons. First, victory in war goes to the side that can best mobilize its resources. As a result, in modern warfare, belligerents resort to any and all means to summon the resources necessary for victory. Second, governments tend to opt for the most practical methods to finance war expenses. With taxation being unpopular, the preferred route often involves printing money. As the Roman statesman Cicero once said, "The sinews of war are infinite money."[15]

This pattern has been observed again and again throughout history. In a process called debasement, empires would create more coins out of thin air by collecting, melting, and then re-minting them at lower concentrations of the base metal (e.g., gold). During the Crisis of the Third Century in Ancient Rome, emperors debased their currency called the denarius.[13] The Byzantines under Constantine IX Monomachos debased the nomisma to fund a war against the Pechenegs.[16] French monarchs during the Hundred Years' War debased the livre.[17] The British Crown suspended the convertibility of the pound sterling to gold during the Napoleonic Wars.[18] During the birth of the United States, the Continental Congress began printing money called continentals to fund the Revolutionary War. Later, in 1862, Congress passed the Legal Tender Act to print paper money called greenbacks to fund the Civil War.[19] The list goes on. History shows that nations devalue their currencies to fund wars and will continue to do so as long as public faith in government-issued money endures.

However, World War I stood apart economically from all previous wars in one fundamental way. It marked the first global conflict where countries could instantly debase their currency by printing more paper money instead of re-minting coins. This newfound power to print money without the constraint of a commodity was too irresistible for countries to turn down. Following World War I, several countries, including Great Britain, attempted to restore the gold exchange rates previously in place. These attempts were short-lived, however, as the world had begun a departure from commodity money entirely. This decoupling of money and tangible assets, as will be explored in the next chapter, was a process that lasted some 50 years.

CHAPTER 4

———•———

CHANGING WORLD ORDER

It was December 1920, two years after the end of World War I, and the factory workers in Highland Park were in high spirits. State-of-the-art industrial facilities dominated this bustling, diverse suburb, located just six miles north of downtown Detroit, with the Ford Motor Company's main factory as its crown jewel.

The factory workers were notably well-compensated. In 1914, Henry Ford initiated the groundbreaking policy of paying his employees $5 per day. This wage was substantially higher than the national minimum and approximately double the average salary of auto workers. Further, production of the Ford Model T was booming. That December, the 800,000th "Tin Lizzie" rolled off the assembly line, nearly doubling the production figures of 1919.[1]

The success of Ford was not an isolated case in the American automotive industry. Emerging car manufacturers, including Chevrolet and Buick, also contributed to the significant growth of production during this era. An industrial boom resonated throughout the country, with Detroit emerging as America's fourth-largest city and on a trajectory to become the nation's wealthiest in the ensuing decades.[2]

Ford Model Ts filled the streets of Detroit, Michigan, in 1920.[3]

Detroit's newfound prosperity was emblematic of a more significant trend, for America in the early 20th century had risen to become the world's manufacturing powerhouse, driven by a multitude of tailwinds. Most notably, the nation experienced a surge in population, crossing the milestone of 100 million citizens in 1915.[4] This growing populace provided a vast pool of workers ready to fuel the industrial expansion. Moreover, the United States was exceptionally blessed with natural resources. In 1920, it was the world's leading oil producer, accounting for over two-thirds of the globe's oil production.[5] Additionally, the US had ascended to the forefront of steel production, which experienced a two-hundredfold increase since 1870.[6]

Lastly, unlike many European nations deeply scarred by World War I, the United States remained largely unscathed by the conflict's direct destruction. This empowered the US to lend its money to European nations ravaged by the war, solidifying its transition from a debtor to a creditor nation. This marked a significant step in the relocation of the world's financial epicenter from London to New York. Together, these factors not only established the United States as the central hub of global manufacturing but also marked the beginning of its rise as a leading financial power and eventual issuer of the world's reserve currency.

The Rise of the US Dollar

Unlike European currencies, the US dollar remained redeemable in gold over the course of World War I.[7] As a result, international trust in the dollar not only endured, but was strengthened during this period. Economic growth in the United States laid the groundwork for it to gradually emerge as a global superpower, a status it would fully consolidate by the end of World War II.

In the past, a country ascending to superpower status came hand in hand with the privilege of issuing the world's reserve currency, as was the case with the Spanish, the Dutch, and, more recently, the British.* Before World War I, the British pound sterling was the undisputed reserve currency, reflecting Britain's dominance as a global superpower. However, the enormous debts accumulated during World War I, coupled with rampant inflation and a loss of trust in British institutions, signaled the beginning of a shift away from the pound sterling's preeminent position.

The post-1918 world was drastically different from the gold standard years before the war. The world economy had globalized, fueled by industrial advancements such as the steamship, railroads, and manufacturing at scale. Oil became a critical global commodity by accelerating global trade and powering the growing industrial bases of every major economy. During this time, money evolved to serve this globalized economy by existing predominantly as

---

* Reserve currency: a globally recognized currency used for the majority of the world's international trade and investments. Many commodities, such as oil and gold, are priced in the reserve currency.

accounting entries on banks' balance sheets to power high-speed transactions rather than in physical form. In this new economic landscape, it became increasingly clear that physical gold was no longer fit to serve its historical role as the primary form of saving and transacting.

Having abandoned the gold standard during World War I, European powers found it challenging to revert to convertibility, as their economies were weakened and inundated with paper currency. These countries had lost much of their gold reserves in funding their war efforts and, as a result, were simply incapable of returning to any commodity standard. Additionally, from the perspective of national governments, the prospect of exercising complete control over the creation of money became an irresistibly compelling option.

Concurrently, there was mounting pressure for the United States to leave the gold standard. With the dollar as the only remaining major currency backed by gold at the end of the war, its value in relation to other European currencies surged, disrupting international trade and exacerbating the inflation felt in Europe. Devaluing the dollar against gold was a viable way to support the economies of Britain and France, bringing the dollar more closely in line with the value of the pound and franc. Further, devaluing the dollar's gold backing would provide a short-term boost to the American economy by stimulating spending and exports, given that a dollar devaluation would make American products cheaper on the international market.

Instead of leaving the gold standard outright, the US Federal Reserve* supported its European allies by lowering interest rates,** thereby stimulating the global economy. To achieve this policy, between 1924 and 1927, the Fed made "substantial" open-market purchases of bonds—equivalent to money printing, or what Federal Reserve members today call "quantitative easing"—in what would be the first of many such policies over the following century.[8] This "easy money" policy supported American business by lowering the cost of borrowing, thereby encouraging debt-fueled spending. This period, known as the Roaring Twenties, was remembered for its booming business,

---

* The US Federal Reserve is the central bank of the United States. First created in 1913, it manages the nation's monetary policy and has three core objectives: maximize employment, stabilize prices, and moderate long-term interest rates.

** Interest rate: Also known as the federal funds rate, the target interest rate is the rate at which banks borrow and lend money to each other. Lowering this rate makes borrowing money cheaper, generally boosting the economy.

soaring stock market, and wild levels of financial speculation—where traders placed increasingly risky bets on financial assets.

As with all debt-fueled business cycles, the Roaring Twenties eventually came to an end in 1929 with the crash of the stock market. In the years that followed, the US economy would find itself in a state of freefall, reeling from a banking crisis, the worst bear market in US history, and the onset of a prolonged economic depression. Nearly four years after the initial stock market crash, it would be this confluence of financial calamities that ultimately compelled the United States to move away from the gold standard under the leadership of Franklin Delano Roosevelt.

Upon assuming office on March 4, 1933, President Roosevelt faced the most severe economic downturn in US history. With unemployment affecting nearly a quarter of the workforce, approximately 13 million Americans were jobless, and there was a marked decrease in wages, salaries, and production. Roosevelt had taken the reins of power from Herbert Hoover, a Republican with a firm belief in limited government intervention. Hoover had presided over the American economy since the stock market crash of 1929 and had done little to address the economic crisis at hand. The public had turned against Hoover as the recession deepened into a depression and was eager for a new leader who would take swift and decisive action.

The day following his inauguration, Roosevelt initiated a four-day banking holiday to halt ongoing bank runs,[*] marking the beginning of a series of assertive measures taken in 1933 to revive the economy. In the process, these actions also significantly transformed the US monetary system.

On April 5, 1933, Roosevelt issued Executive Order 6102, requiring American citizens to give up all their gold possessions in exchange for US dollars, thereby outlawing private gold ownership (with small exceptions such as gold wedding rings and artificial teeth). This executive action was not just symbolic; it was a strategic maneuver to consolidate gold reserves at America's central bank, the Federal Reserve.

---

[*] A bank run occurs when many customers of a bank attempt to withdraw their funds at the same time out of fear that the bank will go insolvent (i.e., bankrupt).

POSTMASTER: PLEASE POST IN A CONSPICUOUS PLACE.—JAMES A. FARLEY, Postmaster General

UNDER EXECUTIVE ORDER OF THE PRESIDENT

Issued April 5, 1933

all persons are required to deliver

ON OR BEFORE MAY 1, 1933

all GOLD COIN, GOLD BULLION, AND GOLD CERTIFICATES now owned by them to a Federal Reserve Bank, branch or agency, or to any member bank of the Federal Reserve System.

Executive Order

FORBIDDING THE HOARDING OF GOLD COIN, GOLD BULLION AND GOLD CERTIFICATES

Executive Order 6102.[9]

Then, over the following year, the Roosevelt administration took steps to detach the US dollar from the gold standard as part of a broader strategy to allow for increased government intervention in the economy. The Gold Reserve Act of 1934 prohibited institutions from exchanging dollars for gold and increased the official price of gold from $20.67 to $35 per ounce, representing a 40% devaluation of the dollar.[10] This act was highly controversial, as it was seen as a betrayal to the American people. Most Americans had willingly given up their gold just months earlier, considering it a patriotic duty. However, the sharp rise in the price of gold shortly after leaving the gold standard meant that Americans who were forced to give up their gold had effectively lost $14 per ounce, equivalent to more than $300 per ounce today.[11] Understandably, many believed such actions by the government unconstitutionally violated personal property rights. Despite these concerns, the Supreme Court upheld the legality of the order, albeit with a narrow margin and several dissenting justices.[11]

The combination of Executive Order 6102 with the subsequent removal of the dollar's gold backing gave the federal government significant leeway to increase spending. Roosevelt had managed to consolidate much of the nation's gold into the hands of the government—a government that no longer had an obligation to meet redemptions of US dollars for gold. This allowed the federal government to engage in deficit spending more freely, unfettered by the limitations of a gold standard.

This increase in spending was a cornerstone of Roosevelt's New Deal—a series of programs, public work projects, financial reforms, and regulations enacted in the United States. The New Deal aimed to provide immediate economic relief, foster recovery, and introduce reforms to mitigate the worst elements of the Great Depression.

President Roosevelt's economic strategies, notably his bold move to abandon the gold standard and the introduction of the comprehensive New Deal reforms, were pivotal in reinvigorating the US economy during the depths of the Great Depression. While subject to criticism for the potential long-term impacts of moving away from a commodity-backed currency, these policies proved highly effective in stimulating immediate economic growth and recovery. Such is the role that path dependence plays in the evolution of money. Following World War I, a series of pragmatic political decisions, not always designed to optimally promote the role of money, shaped the dollar's fate.

It was during this period between World War I and II that the United States cemented its status as a global superpower. The size of the American economy was already vast, surpassing Great Britain in 1872.[12] It shifted from being a debtor to a creditor nation during World War I, as US exports increased threefold. Despite the crippling effects of the Great Depression, the United States' long-term trajectory of economic growth remained unchanged. This resilience can be credited to technological innovations such as Henry Ford's revolution in automobile production, significant population growth, and America's increasingly influential involvement on the world stage, factors that collectively diminished Great Britain's relative economic dominance.

World War II marked a period of accelerated economic expansion for the United States. Between

1939 and 1945, the US economy nearly doubled, driven mainly by the demands of wartime manufacturing and extensive exports to Allied nations. Initially adopting a support role in the conflict, akin to its approach during World War I, the United States managed to protect its economy from the direct devastation of the war, largely occurring outside its borders. The culmination of World War II left little doubt regarding the United States' position as the preeminent global superpower. This period not only solidified the US as the dominant force in international affairs, but also established the US dollar as the principal reserve currency globally, symbolizing the nation's unparalleled economic and geopolitical influence.

The Bretton Woods System

In the aftermath of World War II, the global economy was in turmoil. European nations were ravaged, and all major players had abandoned the conventional gold standard which had been temporarily reinstated by many in the interwar period. The United Kingdom had spent about 25% of its national wealth on the war, and France's industrial and agricultural production plummeted to just 40% of its pre-war levels.[13,14] There was a widely recognized need for a new monetary framework to reconstruct and stabilize the post-war global economy.

In July 1944, 44 countries convened in the quaint New Hampshire town of Bretton Woods to formalize the details of a new global monetary system. The meeting—which came to be known as the Bretton Woods Conference—sought to establish a new reserve currency framework to provide stability to a war-torn world grappling with rampant inflation and dwindling confidence in national currencies. The United States, emerging economically stronger from World War II and holding a major share of the world's gold reserves, saw the conference as a critical opportunity to establish its financial leadership. The relative economic stability of the US during the war and its significant gold reserves provided it with substantial leverage in the conference negotiations, especially since international trade deficits were still settled in gold.[15] Additionally, the US was formulating what would become the Marshall Plan, designed to financially assist war-torn European nations. The US used the allure of this aid as a bargaining chip, making acceptance of its proposed monetary system a prerequisite for receiving Marshall Plan assistance.[16]

The Bretton Woods Conference ultimately produced a resolution that would return the world to a quasi-gold standard and establish a system that would place the US dollar at its center. The dollar was made convertible to gold at $35/oz, while all other world currencies were fixed to the dollar. The International Monetary Fund (IMF) and the World Bank were established as part of this plan to help enforce the system and provide aid to foreign nations. This setup sought to promote international monetary cooperation and reinstate some semblance of a monetary system with natural checks and balances. The system was finalized in 1946, cementing the United States as the new issuer of the world's reserve currency.

In the years following World War II, the US found itself in an ideal position to project power and influence globally, as it was now positioned at the center of the world's new monetary system. This status allowed the US government to engage in significant deficit spending without immediate repercussions. Normally, a country that spends beyond its means and accumulates significant debt risks devaluing its currency, which can lead to inflation and a crisis of confidence among currency holders. But as the issuer of the world's reserve currency, the US now had an "exorbitant privilege,"[17] as France's Finance Minister

Valéry Giscard described. Because the dollar was now the dominant currency used in international trade, there was a consistent and strong demand for it globally.[15] This demand allowed the US government to raise more money to fund government expenditures by issuing debt in the form of Treasury bonds, which were highly sought after by both domestic and international investors. In short, the Bretton Woods system gave the United States an unparalleled borrowing capacity.

With this enhanced fiscal capability, the US implemented a series of "guns and butter" policies during the 1950s and 1960s to expand its global reach. This strategy commenced with President Truman's enactment of the Marshall Plan in 1948, which allocated $13.3 billion over four years for economic assistance to Europe.[18] From 1950 to 1953, the US engaged in the Korean War, incurring expenditures of $30 billion over the duration of the conflict.[19] Additionally, starting in 1947, the US initiated various Cold War military programs, amounting to several hundred billion dollars by the end of the war.[20] To put this into perspective, the United States' total budget in 1950 was $41.9 billion.[21]

Spending continued in the 1960s under President Lyndon B. Johnson's "Great Society" social programs, the Apollo program, and the war in Vietnam. The

Vietnam War signified the true power of the United States' position as the issuer of the world's currency, for it was the first war funded by the United States almost entirely on credit.[15] The war cost $111 billion, topping the already significant spending of years past.[19]

As the US pursued these expansive programs, its deficit continued to grow, putting the health of the Bretton Woods system into question. Whenever the US ran a budget deficit, it effectively increased the amount of dollars in circulation, which were backed by a fixed supply of gold that remained at the same exchange rate of $35/oz. This created a growing imbalance that put into question the ability of the US to meet redemptions with gold. By the late 1960s, it was evident that the system could not be sustained for long. In the words of Niall Ferguson:

> In the late 1960s, US public sector deficits were negligible by today's standards, but large enough to prompt complaints from France that Washington was exploiting its reserve currency status to collect seigniorage* from

---

* Seigniorage: If it costs 10 cents to produce a $1 bill, the seigniorage is 90 cents, or the difference between the value of money and the cost to produce it. Seigniorage is almost always revenue for the government, because the production cost is

America's foreign creditors by printing dollars, much as medieval monarchs had exploited their monopoly on minting to debase the currency.[22]

Alongside France, other major European countries, particularly Britain and Germany, started to question the dollar's role as the reserve currency. They exchanged their dollar reserves for gold, exacerbating the discrepancy between the amount of dollars in circulation and the gold purportedly underpinning it.

By 1971, the outflow of gold from the United States had escalated to alarming levels, with just $11 billion in gold backing $24 billion in dollars.[23] In May of that year, Germany decisively stepped away from the system, decoupling its currency from the dollar. Requests for gold redemption were pouring in from countries worldwide; the British government, for example, told the United States that it wished to withdraw its $3 billion of gold then held in Fort Knox.[24]

It was in this context that in early August 1971, French President Georges Pompidou sent a French naval vessel to New York Harbor with orders to retrieve

---

usually well below the money's face value. Economists often refer to seigniorage as the "inflation tax."

France's gold reserves from the New York Federal Reserve Bank. This action directly challenged the United States' hegemony over the world's money, marking a pivotal moment in global political tensions. The system was on the brink of collapse.

The situation culminated on August 15, 1971, when President Richard Nixon announced the suspension of the dollar's convertibility into gold altogether, an event now known as the "Nixon Shock." This decision put an end to the Bretton Woods system, severing the last ties to the gold standard and ushering in a new era in global monetary policy.

CHAPTER 5

THE FIAT STANDARD

The money we use today, and the broader monetary system often taken for granted, was established following the Nixon Shock of 1971. For the first time in history, global money was entirely detached from any physical backing, introducing an era of fiat money, where money was ordained by government decree alone. The term "fiat" is derived from Latin, literally translating to "by decree." Thus, fiat money is currency that holds value not because of its intrinsic worth, but based on government compulsion.

President Nixon's decision to remove the dollar's gold backing was a necessary response to the mounting economic challenges accumulated over the preceding decades, albeit one laden with significant implications for the future. By removing gold convertibility in 1971, Nixon succeeded in preventing the government's gold coffers from emptying. Further, Nixon restored America's wealth advantage over other countries' reserves by revaluing gold. Detaching the dollar from gold shook the global economy and drastically inflated gold prices. This increased the value of US gold reserves while devaluing the dollar reserves of foreign nations that no longer had gold backing. This shift reallocated wealth, benefiting the gold-rich US to the detriment of poorer, gold-deficient countries. The Nixon Shock serves as another example of path dependence at work, where the dollar depegged from gold, not as a way to improve long-term prosperity, but out of short-term geopolitical and economic necessities.

Following the Nixon Shock, the United States continued to assert its dominance as a global superpower, but the future of the US dollar as the world's reserve currency remained uncertain. This was a unique historical moment; for the first time, an existing global reserve currency sought to uphold its status without being backed by a tangible asset—operating purely as a fiat currency. If successful, this transition would grant the federal government unprecedented financial authority, as it could now spend and create money unbound by the constraints of the Bretton Woods system or a pure gold standard. To ensure the success of this transformation, President Nixon had to build trust both within the United States and on an international scale.

Now that the dollar lacked intrinsic value, foreigners needed a stronger incentive to hold and transact in a fiat currency issued by the United States. Lyn Alden describes this dilemma in her article, *The Fraying of the Petrodollar System*:

> A fiat currency can face particular problems when trying to be used outside of its home country. Why should businesses and governments in other countries accept pieces of paper, which can be printed endlessly by a foreign government and have no firm backing, as a form of payment for their valuable goods and services? Without a real backing, what is it worth? Why would you sell oil to foreigners for paper?
>
> We think of this as normal now, but this five decade period of global fiat currency is unusual and unique in the historical sense. Imagine trying to architect a way to make an all-fiat currency system work on the global stage for the first time in human history. In doing so, you have to somehow convince or force the whole world to trade valuable things for foreign pieces of paper with no guarantee from the paper-issuing governments that those papers are worth anything in particular,

in relation to an amount of gold or other hard assets.[1]

To make this system a success, President Nixon tapped his Secretary of the Treasury, William Simon, to engage in some unconventional diplomacy with none other than Saudi Arabia. Simon, a Wall Street veteran lacking experience in international relations, was tasked with brokering a crucial deal with the Saudis centered on the US dollar—such a deal would be kept secret for more than 40 years.

The US-Saudi meeting was held during the summer of 1974, a period of geopolitical turmoil in the Middle East, which had endured the Yom Kippur War less than a year prior. An oil embargo from Saudi-led OPEC, which targeted the US and other Western nations, had been put in place as a result of the war. The result was a quadrupling of oil prices in a matter of months, leading to high inflation and economic recession across the globe. US-Saudi relations were at a low point, and something needed to change.[2]

After a secret four-day trip to the Saudi port city of Jeddah and several follow-up meetings, the deal that emerged between Saudi Arabia and the United States laid the groundwork for the current global monetary system. Journalist Andrea Wong, who first broke the story in a 2016 Bloomberg article titled *The Untold*

Story Behind Saudi Arabia's 41-Year U.S. Debt Secret,
summarizes the deal's essence:

> The basic framework was strikingly simple.
> The United States would buy oil from Saudi
> Arabia and provide the kingdom military aid
> and equipment. In return, the Saudis would
> plow billions of their petrodollar revenue
> back into Treasuries and finance America's
> spending.[2]

The deal turned out to be a no-brainer—a win-win for
both sides. Saudi Arabia benefited greatly from its
newfound access to military aid from the world's
superpower. A sweetener was the US's commitment to
safeguarding the Strait of Hormuz. This strait, a
slender and geopolitically crucial waterway situated
between Oman and Iran, is a critical juncture through
which approximately one-fifth of the world's oil supply
traverses en route to global markets.[3]

For the United States, the deal represented a much-
needed solidification of the dollar's reserve currency
status following the Nixon Shock of 1971. A key
element was that the Saudis agreed to sell all their oil
in US dollars—a policy not limited to transactions
with the US but applicable to all of its trading partners.
This meant that any country wishing to purchase Saudi

oil would first need to acquire US dollars to make the purchase. Seeing the benefits reaped by Saudi Arabia in the form of military protection, all other OPEC* nations followed this same strategy by the following year, requiring oil purchases to be made in US dollars. Given that oil is the most important commodity from both a geopolitical and economic standpoint and that these nations collectively reside over nearly 80% of the world's oil reserves, this exclusive use of the US dollar for oil transactions effectively enforced the dollar's role as the primary currency for international trade and as a global store of value.[4]

Within short order, the rest of the developed world woke up to this new reality: Holding US dollars was imperative to actively engage in the burgeoning global economy. As compensation, the United States was positioned and willing to assume the mantle of protector of international trade routes, a role essential for the sustenance of this new economic order. Thus, America's informal role of global military policeman, guardian of trade routes and allied territory, had begun.

---

* OPEC: The Organization of the Petroleum Exporting Countries, originally founded in 1960 by Iran, Iraq, Kuwait, Saudi Arabia, and Venezuela. Today it is made up of 13 countries.

In reciprocation for America's military oversight and the stability it provided, nations worldwide reinforced the value of the US dollar, using it for trade invoicing and as a staple in their central bank reserves. This practice meant that a significant portion of the international savings accumulated by countries worldwide would be channeled into US government securities—essentially loans to the US government— thereby supporting the expanding US fiscal deficits. By 1975, nearly half of all money held by foreign powers were in US dollars, marking the dawn of an era dominated by fiat money.[5]

The ascension of the United States to unparalleled monetary dominance with a fiat currency was akin to wielding a monetary superweapon. By building a system where the global economy relied upon dollars to conduct trade, the US created an environment where fiat money was in persistent demand to hold in reserves and savings internationally. The cherry on top was that the dollar was no longer constrained by a gold backing. This enabled the US to engage in deficit spending without facing any traditional constraints or negative political repercussions.

US government bonds sold to a global market financed America's deficit spending. These were purchased not only by Saudi Arabia as part of the deal structured with the US, but also by the entire world. Foreign powers now needed to hold dollars to conduct international trade, and US government bonds, a form of dollar-denominated savings, proved to be the best mechanism to do so. For the US government, this ability to spend beyond its means has persisted to this day, permitting the US to run budget deficits for nearly the entirety of the past five decades.

A New Economy

This new model, centered on fiat money, gave rise to a transformative shift in the American economic system, marking a departure from its mid-20th-century success as an export-driven manufacturing powerhouse. The American economy transitioned toward a landscape dominated by consumerism and heavily reliant on debt.

One immediate consequence of America's dominant monetary status was a significant alteration in its trade balance,* increasingly favoring imports (see chart below). As the US dollar strengthened against other currencies due to high global demand, this shift manifested in two ways. First, it lowered the cost of

---

* A country's trade balance is the difference between how much it produces (exports) and how much it consumes (imports).

imported goods for American consumers, boosting import levels. Second, it raised the prices of American products on the international market, diminishing the appeal of US goods abroad.

The United States' balance of trade since the 1960s. Since 1971, the US has had a chronic negative balance, meaning it imports more goods and services than it exports.[6]

The relative rise in the value of the US dollar presented challenges for American manufacturers and exporters. In an increasingly competitive global market, US manufacturers who wanted to remain profitable were faced with a trade-off: move their production overseas to take advantage of lower labor and manufacturing costs, or keep their production within the US while suppressing American workers' wages to remain competitive with the global labor market.

Thus, the production of iconic American products experienced a wholesale decline of extreme proportions. American manufacturers of automobiles, apparel, and appliances increasingly elected to move their production overseas in search of lower labor costs. Between 1998 and 2020, the United States witnessed the closure of 70,000 factories, leading to the loss of five million manufacturing jobs.[7] Over the last decade, despite ongoing plant shutdowns in the US, car manufacturers have increasingly embraced the benefits of foreign production, with vehicle imports from Mexico rising by over 6% annually.[8]

This shift has profoundly affected the American blue-collar workforce, who have either lost jobs due to the relocation of production or face stagnant wages in the increasingly competitive global market. The accompanying chart shows the start of this trend in 1971: While productivity continues to rise, hourly compensation in the US has remained largely unchanged.[6]

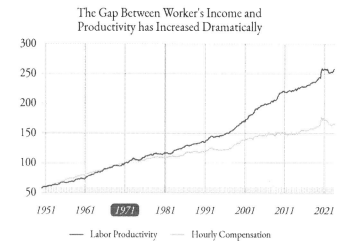

The Gap Between Worker's Income and Productivity has Increased Dramatically

Since 1971, increases in labor productivity have outpaced growth in hourly compensation, representing a real decrease in workers' wages over time (Labor productivity, defined as output per hour, and hourly compensation, are normalized to 100 in 1971).[6]

Concurrent with this shift in trade and manufacturing, the American economy developed a taste for debt. The ability of the federal government to borrow cheaply trickled down through the economy, enabling Wall Street and Main Street to do the same. This trend saw financial institutions and individuals alike embracing more readily available borrowing options, reflecting a broader shift in the nation's financial behavior.

Home mortgages, credit cards, financial derivatives, and car loans became embedded in the American economy during this era. The boom in debt-linked products spurred a remarkable expansion of the financial services sector, which tripled in size relative to the rest of the economy between 1950 and 2010.[9] Once perceived as a dormant industry, Wall Street flourished and profited immensely, inspiring the narratives found in movies and books such as *The Wolf of Wall Street* and *Liar's Poker*.

A notable highlight from the 1970s was the emergence of the junk bond market. Junk bonds, also known as high-yield or speculative bonds, are issued by companies with low credit ratings (at a higher risk of bankruptcy) looking to borrow money. By purchasing bonds, investors effectively lend money to these high-risk companies and, in return, receive a higher return on investment. Mirroring the national trend toward debt, the junk bond market saw rapid growth under the fiat dollar system, ballooning from $10 billion in 1979 to $189 billion in 1989.[10]

Attracted by the potential for high returns, investors gravitated toward junk bonds despite the greater likelihood of default (failure of the company to repay the loan). Meanwhile, borrowers eagerly amassed debt to fund ambitious corporate finance ventures such as restructurings* and leveraged buyouts.** The 1980s witnessed a surge in corporate takeovers and buyouts, often financed with junk bonds.

In 1989, RJR Nabisco, a prominent manufacturer known for Oreo cookies, Ritz Crackers, and Camel cigarettes, became a high-profile casualty of the junk bond craze. That year, a private equity firm named KKR executed a hostile takeover of the company, acquiring it for $25 billion. Notably, KKR used little of its own money for the purchase, about 5% of the final purchase price, financing the remainder through junk bonds and similar means. Following the leveraged buyout playbook, KKR swiftly implemented cost-cutting measures, including significant layoffs, to reduce expenses and boost profitability. Ultimately, KKR's investment didn't yield the expected returns, and RJR Nabisco, once a manufacturing giant, was left

---

* Restructuring refers to the process of significantly altering the structure, operations, or finances of a company. This can involve changes such as mergers and acquisitions, divestitures, changes in ownership, reorganization of legal structure, downsizing, or cost-cutting measures.

** A leveraged buyout is a financial transaction where a company is purchased primarily with borrowed funds. Leveraged buyouts are typically executed by private equity firms and involve significant amounts of debt, with the expectation that the acquired company's cash flow will cover the loan repayments.

in tatters. The KKR-RJR Nabisco deal serves as a microcosm of an American economy becoming increasingly financialized, where financial gains frequently came to the detriment of blue-collar workers.[11]

In essence, the post-1971 American economy reoriented around the US dollar, shifting away from its previous foundation in the American working class. This economic structure favors those in higher income brackets in sectors such as finance, government, healthcare, and technology. These individuals reap the rewards of globalization and dollarization without facing their adverse effects. Conversely, those in lower income brackets, particularly workers in manufacturing, find themselves at a disadvantage because their jobs are more prone to outsourcing and automation. This shift in economic focus and the resulting job displacement has significantly contributed to today's wealth and income inequality, fostering a system that fails to support the average American. The chart below exemplifies this widening of income inequality. While the wages of the 95th percentile continued to increase at a normal rate following 1971, the incomes of the 20th percentile remained stagnant.[12]

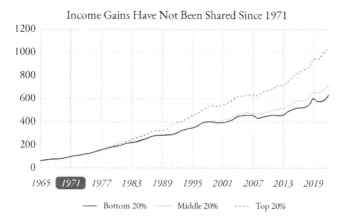

Income Gains Have Not Been Shared Since 1971

Since 1971, the top 20% of US families saw a far greater rise in their incomes than the middle and bottom 20%, representing an increase in income inequality. (Nominal income normalized to 100 in 1971)[12]

The net effect of the post-1971 fiat economy is best described by economists Yakov Feygin and Dominik Leusder:

[Global] Dollar [supremacy] feeds a growing American trade deficit that shifts the country's economy toward the accumulation of rents rather than the growth of productivity. This has contributed to a falling labor [...] share of income, and to the ballooning cost of services such as education, medical care, and rental housing.[13]

Debt-Fueled Growth

The privilege of the federal government to borrow and spend at an artificially low cost has now persisted for more than half a century. In theory, this privilege can be sustained as long as the US dollar remains the global reserve currency. The rationale behind this is straightforward: With a substantial global base of individuals and institutions holding dollars for trade and savings, the US federal government can leverage this widespread reliance on its currency by deficit spending without facing repercussions. A virtuous cycle is thus created, where the demand for dollars helps maintain low borrowing costs for the US, whose deficit spending on military operations and other global aid programs reinforces the dollar's central role in the international financial system.

However, the past few decades have shown signs of an unreliable system. The United States economy, which once derived a significant benefit from the ability to take on debt, is now experiencing the consequences of this burden. Since 1971, the federal government's debt has grown over three times faster than the economy, skyrocketing by 78 times (as shown in the chart below).[6]

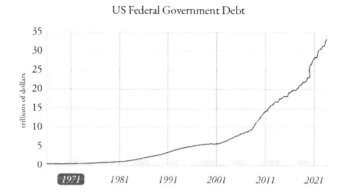

US Federal Government Debt

Since 1971, US Federal Debt has increased exponentially, a rate that is not sustainable in the long run.[6]

Who owns America's debt? Unlike most foreign countries, whose debt is predominantly owned by their citizens, the United States has borrowed increasingly from foreigners looking for places to invest their US dollar surpluses. This trend is evident in the US's net international investment position, which reflects the disparity between American assets owned by foreigners and foreign assets held by Americans. This gap has widened to over $18 trillion, as illustrated in the accompanying chart. One manifestation of this trend is the visible increase of foreign ownership of real estate in America's coastal cities, linked to the ongoing federal trade and budget deficits.[6]

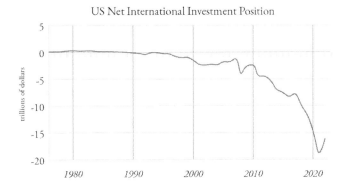

US Net International Investment Position

Over the last two decades, the US net international investment position has continued to decrease, representing larger foreign ownership of US assets such as real estate.[6]

When Americans own a smaller share of domestic assets and the federal government has a more considerable debt burden, the American economy is left more vulnerable to systemic shocks. In this context, business failures, traditionally viewed as a natural aspect of economic cycles marked by creative destruction,* now pose a risk to the stability of the entire system.

The fragility of the American economy became apparent to the world in 2008, when a financial crisis

---

* Creative destruction refers to the process whereby old, outdated industries and technologies are dismantled and replaced by new, innovative ones, driving economic growth and advancements despite causing temporary disruptions or job losses. This concept highlights the inherent dynamism and evolutionary progress within capitalist economies.

arose due to decades of such excessive financialization and leverage, particularly in the market for home mortgages. The collapse of Lehman Brothers, a Wall Street giant with $639 billion in assets,[14] marked the largest bankruptcy in US history. Similarly, the investment bank Bear Stearns crumbled under the weight of a highly leveraged portfolio of mortgage-backed securities. The US government, recognizing the likelihood of total economic collapse if no immediate interventions were taken, responded with unprecedented bailout measures. The most significant was the Troubled Asset Relief Program (TARP), authorized by Congress in October 2008. TARP equipped the government with $700 billion to purchase distressed assets, particularly mortgage-backed securities, and to inject capital into struggling financial institutions. This move aimed to stabilize the banking sector and restore confidence in the financial system—in the short term.

Over time, the economy has grown increasingly vulnerable, a trend illustrated by the escalating scale of bailouts required to stabilize systemic shocks. While the 2008 bailouts were once considered unprecedented in magnitude, they pale in comparison to the size and frequency of subsequent government interventions. In 2012, the Federal Reserve launched a significant monetary stimulus, injecting over $1.6 trillion of new money into the economy over two years to foster economic activity—a sum surpassing any individual bailout effort of 2008.

In early 2020, as the COVID-19 pandemic spread globally, the fragility of the US economy once again came to the fore. The considerable amount of pre-existing debt within the economy made it impractical to demand a halt to economic activity without providing enormous stimulus. Continuous financial commitments such as interest payments persisted, and the need for businesses to remain running was imperative.

To address these issues, the US government implemented a wide range of bailouts and stimulus programs. On April 3, 2020, the federal government began issuing loans to small businesses to help keep employees on payroll. As of October 2023, the program issued 11.5 million loans, totaling $792 billion, a majority of which was forgiven.[15] Later, on April 11, 2020, the US government deposited $1,200 into the bank accounts of some 160 million Americans, totaling $292 billion. The total fiscal expenditure of these and other measures exceeded $4 trillion, over six times larger than the measures taken in 2008.[17]

The chart below depicts the extent to which fiscal (government spending) and monetary (money creation) stimuli have increased from crisis to crisis. The 2020 COVID-19 relief measures, implemented to meet an urgent short-term economic need within a context of ongoing fiscal deficits, inadvertently magnified economic instability and fueled inflation in the long term. This effect will be further explained in the next chapter.

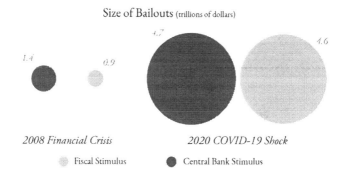

Size of Bailouts (trillions of dollars)

2008 Financial Crisis   *2020 COVID-19 Shock*

Fiscal Stimulus   Central Bank Stimulus

The stimulus deployed in reaction to COVID-19 dwarfed the stimulus used to mitigate the 2008 financial crisis.[16]

Three years after the onset of COVID-19, in yet another testament to the systemic vulnerability of America's economy, the United States faced another crisis with the looming collapse of regional banks across the nation, including Silicon Valley Bank and First Republic Bank. These institutions were on the brink of failure, threatening to trigger a broader financial crisis.

Again, following the 2008 playbook, the Federal Reserve took decisive action by lending freshly printed US dollars to banks in need at subsidized rates. This lending program was in effect until March 2024, with the total amount of funds issued by the Federal Reserve reaching as high as $141 billion.[6]

The responses to the crises of 2008, 2020, and 2023, coupled with the continued deficit spending by the US, have grown America's debt burden to a size that cannot reasonably be paid off under any timeframe. Indeed, the government's own budget office now projects America's debt load to double again in relation to the size of the economy by 2050.

It is commonly believed that the frequent bailouts and deficits incurred by the federal government are funded by taxing the American public. In reality, this is not entirely the case. The American tax base is insufficient to cover the nation's debt or current spending needs. Consequently, the federal government increasingly resorts to its authority to print money as a means of financing expenditures. Therefore, besides paying for bailouts and deficits via taxation, the American public must also pay for this spending through the indirect cost of inflation, a more subtle form of taxation that results from the creation of new money that decreases the purchasing power of individuals. By creating new money, the US government is solving a short-term problem while sacrificing the long-term viability of the dollar. Historically, a drop in a currency's scarcity came from the invention of a new technology. In the case of the dollar post-1971, the invention of a new global political arrangement between the US and Saudi Arabia ultimately led to the erosion of its scarcity. As history has repeatedly demonstrated, when the scarcity of a certain currency begins to diminish, it is only a matter of time before it falls out of prominence.

CHAPTER 6

—————◆—————

BROKEN MONEY

By 1992, the US national debt had become a significant concern for American citizens. The federal government had recorded budget deficits for 23 consecutive years, culminating in a total debt load exceeding $4 trillion.[1] Year 1992 ushered in another presidential election, with candidates from both the Republican and Democratic parties running on the idea that rapidly rising debt was a danger to the nation's future. During a CBS interview, third-party candidate Ross Perot notably emphasized this issue with his widely resonating analogy: "The debt is like a crazy aunt we keep down in the basement. All the neighbors know she's there, but nobody wants to talk to her."[2]

Despite widespread agreement on the need for budget reform and fiscal prudence, the existing framework and incentives of the US dollar system made it challenging to alter the long-established fiscal trends that began in 1971. As a result, the federal deficit, which grew sixfold between 1992 and 2023, has remained an issue for the country.[3]

This rise in the nation's debt has fueled prophecies of economic collapse and widespread default for many years. While the continuous and rapid increase of the US debt is unsustainable in the long term, these catastrophic predictions haven't materialized as the US has managed to continue the growth of both its economy and debt burden without yet facing a "great reckoning." An unintuitive reality is that the federal government is unlikely to ever default on its debt. As our system is currently structured, the government doesn't need to tackle its fiscal issues through direct methods, such as spending cuts or tax hikes. Instead, the government can indirectly ease its debt burden by using inflation as a strategy.

Inflation can be thought of as the erosion of the value of money. If the annual inflation rate is 10%, it follows that a dollar will be roughly 10% less valuable in 12 months. The effect of inflation builds over time, implying that even a modest annual rate of 2–5% can significantly reduce the value of money over several decades. Since 1971, the inflation rate in the United States has been moderate, seldom surpassing 5%. This consistent, albeit modest, inflation has caused the dollar to lose more than 85% of its value over 50 years (see the chart below).[1] In practice, this erosion wipes out the value of cash savings and puts an undue burden on the working class to continuously negotiate for salary raises that keep up with rising prices. This degradation of money via inflation equips governments with the ability to reduce their effective debt burdens.

Purchasing Power of the US Dollar

The purchasing power, or the ability to buy a set of goods, of the dollar in US cities (normalized to 100 in 1971).[1]

The power to create new money gives the government the capacity to diminish the value of its debt burden by generating inflation. Those in debt, including the government, benefit from inflation as it reduces the effective cost of repaying debts. When money is devalued, the value of an outstanding debt likewise represents less of a burden.

To understand this approach to debt reduction, let's begin with a simplified example. Brad is a young man who loves throwing lavish parties and fine dining. Unfortunately, Brad lives well beyond his means. After taking on student loans for a bachelor's degree and MBA program, Brad is now $340,000 in debt during what we will call 'Year 1'. To make matters worse, Brad was not a good student and now works a job earning an annual salary of $44,000. Despite this, Brad spends $61,000 a year, with the difference paid with credit card debt. To put it simply, Brad has a serious problem.

It may be hard to believe, but the financial figures of the US government are identical to Brad's... only **100 million times larger.**

Year 1 Budget

Brad		Federal government	
Income	*$44,000*	*Tax Receipts*	*$4,400,000,000,000*
Expenses	*$61,000*	*Spending Outlays*	*$6,100,000,000,000*
Deficit	*-$17,000*	*Deficit*	*-$1,700,000,000,000*
Total Debt	*$340,000*	*Total Debt*	*$34,000,000,000,000*
Debt / Income Ratio	*7.7x*	*Debt / Income Ratio*	*7.7x*

A hypothetical scenario of Brad's income and expenses. The federal government's budget is 100 million times larger than Brad's finances.

Clearly, Brad's behavior is unsustainable, with a debt load seven times higher than his income and increasing every year. What if there was a way to diminish the size of his debt burden, allowing him to continue his lavish lifestyle a little longer?

Enter the power of inflation. Suppose that Brad has a superpower that allows him to dictate what the rate of inflation will be at any given time. Brad decides he wants inflation to be 50% in year two—a high rate indeed. Inflation has the effect of raising Brad's income *and* his expenses by 50%, but critically, *not* the amount of his existing debt burden.

Year 2 Budget

Brad		Federal government	
Income	$66,000	Tax Receipts	$6,600,000,000,000
Expenses	$91,500	Spending Outlays	$9,150,000,000,000
Deficit	-$25,500	Deficit	-$2,550,000,000,000
Total Debt	$365,500	Total Debt	$36,550,000,000,000
Debt / Income Ratio	5.5x	Debt / Income Ratio	5.5x

Brad and the federal government can reduce their relative debt burden by inflating their income and expenses.

Thus, while Brad didn't address his spending habits, the high inflation diminished the size of his debt burden *relative* to his income even though his total debt burden rose by $25,000. Notice how Brad's debt burden is only five times greater than his income in Year 2, compared with seven in Year 1. This effect greatly benefits Brad, as he can continue spending lavishly without worrying about his debt burden growing faster than his income.

Unlike Brad, a make-believe character with an absurd superpower, the federal government finds itself with a high debt burden *and* the ability to create money. As such, it has an irresistible incentive to lean toward this "hidden tax" of inflation to manage its debt rather than using traditional methods. This strategy has been known and implemented throughout history; just after World War I, John Maynard Keynes wrote the following about inflation as an indirect tax:

> By continuing the process of inflation, governments can confiscate, secretly and unobserved, an important part of the wealth of their citizens. By this method they not only confiscate, but they confiscate arbitrarily; and, while the process impoverished many, it actually enriches some.[4]

The federal government's debt currently surpasses $34 trillion, exceeding the total size of the American economy by 25%. One in three tax dollars now goes to interest payments on this debt burden. As the US continues to increase its budget deficits, the gap between government spending and tax revenues will continue to widen. As a result, inflation appears to be the only viable solution to manage this escalating debt.

The Societal Impact of Inflation

For decades, inflation was hardly a concern or a subject of discussion, but this has changed recently. Goods are becoming more expensive noticeably quicker than before, making inflation a prevalent topic of conversation today.

While it may seem as though the inflation experienced in the US is an abnormality, throughout history and around the world today, high inflationary periods have been the norm rather than the exception. In 2021, some 1.2 billion people worldwide lived in countries experiencing double or triple-digit inflation.[5] That same year, citizens of Iran, Lebanon, Syria, Sudan, Zimbabwe, and Venezuela saw the value of their money fall by more than one-third.

In extreme cases, inflation can be so high that it renders money worthless within weeks or months. *Hyperinflation* refers to the phenomenon where prices rise by 50% or more each month. This compounding effect quickly destroys the wealth of anyone holding money. In a world of 50% monthly inflation, a $5 beer today would cost $650 in one year. Venture capitalist and financial writer Nic Carter elaborates on the prevalence of hyperinflation:

> All told, 56 distinct hyperinflation events can be identified in history. All except one took place in the 20th or 21st centuries. The causes have differed and include war, political chaos, and sudden changes in economic regimes. But there is one constant: Each occurred in an economy with a discretionary, fiat monetary standard. No hyperinflation event has ever occurred in an economy where monetary policy was constrained by a commodity standard.[5]

For governments grappling with substantial debt, high inflation can be advantageous in the short-term, serving both as a covert form of taxation and as a means of diminishing the relative burden of their debt. It's important to note that inflation is most readily induced in economies operating on fiat money. Fiat money lacks tangible backing, granting governments enhanced control over the money supply and, consequently, the inflation rate. While this control provides a strategic capability to manage debt, as Nic Carter's quote highlights, this approach has significant long-term economic repercussions.

For society at large, inflation of any magnitude has deleterious effects—it is no different from the whittling away of one of money's core attributes: scarcity. As previously discussed, monies of the past frequently fell out of prominence when their scarcity was compromised. In the case of cowrie shell necklaces, their demise as money occurred when global shipping allowed for rapid inflation of new cowries. For wampum, the introduction of European steel drills significantly reduced the cost of manufacturing wampum from clams, thereby ruining its natural scarcity. Tobacco never had natural scarcity and thus needed artificial constraints enforced by colonial governments to prop it up as legal tender. Such is the case with the US dollar today; eliminating a fixed exchange rate for gold has removed the only natural constraint enforcing the dollar's scarcity. If history is to be our teacher, it follows that just as cowrie shells, wampum, and tobacco all fell due to failures in their scarcity, so too will the US dollar.

While in the long run, a loss of scarcity brings about the demise of a currency, in the medium term, a loss of scarcity manifests in society's loss of trust in said currency. One symptom of this is a reluctance to save for the future; this is self-evident in today's society, awash with unrestricted fiat currency. It is now socially acceptable to take on debt instead of saving up for major expenses such as college, a new car, or a home. Young workers are less inclined to save for retirement, opting for more immediate needs. Signposts of this shift in behavior are seen in the spending patterns of young adults, who are increasingly turning toward leaps of faith, such as meme-stocks, parlays on sporting events, or bets in unknown cryptocurrencies. This is exemplified by the chart below, showing that since 1971, net saving as a percentage of national income has been on a steady decline, meaning that Americans are saving less of their paycheck year after year.[1]

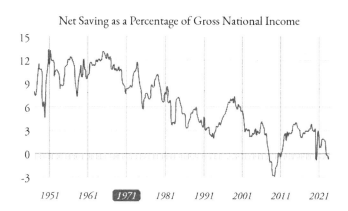

Since 1971, Americans have been saving less year after year, as captured by the Federal Reserve's data showing net saving is becoming a smaller percentage of national income.[1]

These actions are not the result of foolishness. Rather, they are rational responses to a financial environment where conventional saving methods seem less viable. Consider the dramatic 80%* increase in the United States' base money supply in 2020 alone (see chart below).[1] This significant monetary inflation prompts a reevaluation of conventional financial wisdom, guiding individuals toward alternative stores of value.

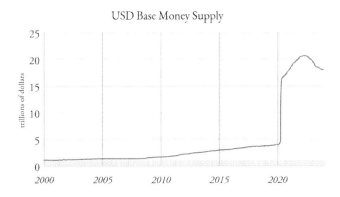

USD Base Money Supply

In 2020, the federal government's stimulus measures in reaction to COVID-19 dramatically increased the money supply, ultimately leading to more inflation.[1]

Such an inflationary currency as the US dollar can lead to many negative second-order consequences, as financial writer Lyn Alden describes:

---

* There are multiple ways of measuring the amount of dollars that circulate in the economy. "Base money," otherwise known as M1, is a measure of the most readily available funds, including physical currency and money in checking accounts. Broader classifications of money, such as M2 and M3, expanded by a lesser amount in the year 2020.

Prices are what allow people to coordinate, and when money supply keeps increasing at such a fast rate, it is highly disruptive for economic coordination. In addition to constantly diluting peoples' liquid savings… this money supply growth constantly dilutes peoples' wages. If they are not aggressively seeking higher wages year after year, they're falling behind in international purchasing power terms. If small businesses are not aggressively raising prices, they're falling behind as well. If landlords are not aggressively raising rents, their real estate investment is unlikely to keep up with international purchasing power.

It's like being on a treadmill at full-speed, trying desperately to keep up. If you aren't aggressively seeking out ways to increase your income and protect your savings, you're getting diluted away. And it's especially harsh for the least financially secure people. They're the ones that often don't have bank accounts, and are dealing with paper cash without even earning interest on their savings that keep devaluing.[7]

Between the diminution of wages, the distortion of societal coordination, the shift from saving to speculation, and countless other symptoms of inflation, the effects add up in a big way, for inflation is the surest way to erode society's trust in its own institutions. In the wake of World War I, when European nations were reeling from the inflationary effects of conflict, John Maynard Keynes wrote the following in his essay *The Economic Consequences of the Peace*:

> There is no subtler, no surer means of overturning the existing basis of society than to debauch the currency. The process engages all the hidden forces of economic law on the side of destruction, and does it in a manner which not one man in a million is able to diagnose.[2]

As shown throughout this book, the key to money's functioning is trust. To remove this key ingredient from the US dollar, a fiat currency that is backed by nothing but trust, is to destine the dollar to the same fate as cowrie shells, wampum, tobacco, and every other failed currency that preceded it.

The End of the US Dollar Reserve System

Throughout history, money has evolved in parallel with society, with the emergent form of money mirroring the needs of society itself. As seen with the dawn of the telegraph at the end of the 19th century, advances in society often lead to evolving monetary requirements. Thus, it follows that when a certain money ceases to meet the demands of society, it gradually phases out and is replaced by a superior alternative. Due to the deep-rooted nature of societal trust systems, such as money, this process can take many decades.

Before the US dollar, it was the British pound that held the title of global reserve currency. The pound rose to prominence in tandem with the British Empire in the 18th century. At the time, the United Kingdom was at the center of the Industrial Revolution, producing many great inventions that would propel its empire to global superpower status. As a result, the pound was unrivaled as a reserve currency for almost two hundred years.

This began to change in earnest during World War I, when Great Britain temporarily ended the pound's convertibility to gold, effectively rendering it a fiat currency. Great Britain's massive debt burden, alongside its damaged economy, forced the government to devalue the pound repeatedly, triggering a period of high inflation. Simultaneously, the world's economic and financial center rapidly shifted from London to New York.

In hindsight, the pound's replacement by the US dollar as a reserve currency was inevitable—even as early as 1920. However, almost five decades passed before the dollar was widely recognized as the global reserve currency. Investor and philanthropist Ray Dalio documents this in detail in his book *Principles for Dealing with the Changing World Order*:

> The decline in the British pound was a protracted affair that involved several significant devaluations. After attempts to make the pound convertible failed in 1946–47, it was devalued by 30 percent against the dollar in 1949. Though this worked in the short term, over the next two decades Britain's declining competitiveness led to repeated balance of payments strains that culminated with the devaluation of 1967... After the devaluation, little faith remained in the pound. Central banks began to sell their [pound] reserves and buy dollars, deutschemarks, and yen, as opposed to simply accumulating fewer pounds in new reserve

holdings. The average share of [pounds] in central bank reserve holdings collapsed within two years.[8]

All the signs existed in 1920 that showed what lay ahead for the British pound: a high debt burden by its issuer, persistently high levels of inflation, and a geopolitical shift in global superpowers. What it took for the change in reserve currency status to finally occur was the passage of time; new generations were born and brought up in a world where it simply made sense to interface in US dollars rather than pounds.

Today, all the signs are in place showing what lies ahead for the US dollar. This is not a prognostication of the United States' future as a global superpower, which may well persist for centuries. After all, although the US dollar replaced the pound, the United Kingdom remains a wealthy and influential country today—its citizens enjoy a high standard of living that has continued to improve throughout time. The reality, however, is that the US dollar no longer meets the demands of the world we live in today.

Internationally, the incentive for both foreign central banks and citizens to hold and transact in dollars is diminishing. The dollar's rapid rate of devaluation makes it less appealing for foreign governments to save their surpluses in US government bonds, as these investments fail to outpace the rate of inflation. When the federal government pays 3% interest on its debt, for example, lending money to the US government is a losing investment whenever the inflation rate exceeds 3%.

The world is moving toward a multi-polar system without a single unchallenged superpower, one where countries increasingly value using their own currencies for trade instead of the US dollar. In a landmark move in November 2023, Saudi Arabia, long considered a cornerstone of the dollar reserve system, formalized a pivotal agreement with China that took steps toward trade using their currency, the renminbi.[9] This decision marked a departure from Saudi Arabia's nearly 50-year policy of exclusively using the US dollar for oil pricing. As human rights activist Alex Gladstein remarks in *Check Your Financial Privilege*:

> More and more countries are denominating oil trade in other currencies, like euros, yuan, and rubles, partly because they fear reliance on a weakening system and partly because the US government continues to use the dollar as a weapon.[10]

This is especially the case for China and Russia; as of 2020, only 33% of Russian exports to China were dollar-based, versus 98% six years ago.[11] Additionally, several other countries, including Brazil, Egypt, India, Iran, Russia, and Turkey, have shown interest or have taken steps to facilitate trade in currencies other than the US dollar.

Recent geopolitical events have highlighted an additional dimension of risk for countries holding US dollars: the possibility of the US government imposing sanctions or penalties that could render their holdings worthless. Russia's invasion of Ukraine in early 2022 is a clear illustration of this risk. The conflict began on February 24, consisting of targeted bombings of the Ukrainian capital of Kyiv and other eastern regions of the country. While the invasion was physically constrained to a small area of Eastern Europe, the global response was significant. In addition to $113 billion in aid and military support[12] given by the US, even greater aid was indirectly provided to Ukraine through America's financial repression of Russia. Not long after the initial invasion, the US Treasury froze more than $300 billion in Russian central bank assets held abroad in American and European banks.[13] This move was unprecedented in both its scale and implications for the US dollar, representing the first time the US dollar had been weaponized against a major power. Traditionally, the US avoided freezing foreign assets to maintain global confidence in the US dollar as a reserve currency; this historical approach encouraged international investment in US government bonds and dollar-based transactions. However, the seizure of Russia's assets signals a shift in American priorities. The reality of today is that, as opposed to 30 years ago, foreigners have little reason to buy into the US dollar reserve system.

A century ago, as the British pound was falling out of prominence, it was clear what would come next as a global reserve currency: The United States was becoming a global superpower, and the US dollar had a nearly 200-year track record of relative stability as a transactable currency. Today, what will replace the dollar as the preeminent reserve asset is less apparent. Furthermore, the demands of society call for a new form of money altogether. In our interconnected world, where interactions and commerce predominantly occur over the internet and social media, traditional financial systems are being reevaluated. Commerce now transcends physical space, operating within the realm of the internet. What comes next as money, therefore, will emerge organically according to the demands and needs of a 21st-century society.

PART III

MONEY OF THE FUTURE

CHAPTER 7

———————————

THE INTERNET OF MONEY

On October 4, 1957, the Soviet Union successfully launched Sputnik 1, the first-ever artificial satellite, into orbit. While an incredible feat of engineering in its own right, this launch was monumental because it was a direct threat to US global hegemony. At the time of the Sputnik launch, the Cold War was at its peak and became a catalyst for increased American innovation. In reaction to the Soviet technological breakthrough in space, the United States decided to prioritize technological advancements and develop a communications system resilient to potential Soviet nuclear attacks. In light of this, President Dwight D. Eisenhower established the Advanced Research Projects Agency (ARPA) in 1958. Composed of leading national scientists, ARPA's mission was to enhance the American military's technological capabilities, ensuring its lead over the Soviet Union and preparing the country for a possible nuclear confrontation. A key initiative of ARPA was the creation of a robust nationwide communication network, a project that laid the groundwork for what we today recognize as the internet.

During this period, computers were largely confined to military scientists and university personnel, primarily because exorbitant costs made them inaccessible to businesses and households. The expensive nature of these machines meant they were few in number, compelling researchers to travel considerable distances to access a single computer. Furthermore, the necessity to accommodate multiple researchers needing its functionalities led to the emergence of "time-sharing." This functionality allowed various researchers to use the computer simultaneously through different terminals. The need for shared access catalyzed the focused development of computer networks.

At the time, scientist Paul Baran was investigating how the US Air Force could maintain command over its fleet in the event of a nuclear attack. In 1964, he proposed an innovative communication system that lacked a central command point, thereby rendering it immune to disablement by a nuclear strike. He envisioned this system as a "distributed network," where each node could communicate with others independently, eliminating reliance on a central hub.

This design significantly reduced the vulnerability to nuclear attacks. Baran's pioneering concept spurred further intensive research in computer networking.

By 1965, the foundational elements of Baran's concept were actualized when research scientist Lawrence Roberts successfully facilitated communication between two computers at different locations, marking a historic first in computer networking. This milestone ignited a cascade of research efforts, resulting in the birth of ARPANET in 1969. By 1973, ARPANET, often regarded as the precursor to the modern internet, linked a diverse array of 30 research, academic, and military institutions across the United States, the United Kingdom, and Norway. This pioneering network enabled communication between all participating entities, thus establishing a new paradigm in the realm of computer-based connectivity.

The internet didn't truly begin its rapid expansion until 1986, more than a decade after ARPANET's inception. In 1986, the internet connected approximately 2,000 systems, surging to 30,000 just a year later. A significant milestone was reached in 1993 when 22-year-old Marc Andreessen developed the world's first web browser, a precursor to modern versions such as Chrome or Safari.[1] This innovation made navigating the internet far more user-friendly, marking the first time users could easily explore the digital realm. Initially, in 1993, the internet hosted just 130 websites, which would skyrocket to over 100,000 three years later, signaling the internet's decisive first step into the mainstream.[1]

Just as the telegraph drastically transformed global communication and commerce in the late 19th century, the advent of the internet roughly a century later has significantly reshaped society. Today, 93% of Americans have access to the internet, spending an average of 11 hours per day consuming digital media across all mediums.[2, 3] Meeting people online is now the most common way for new couples to connect.[4] Furthermore, 86% of Americans now source their news from digital devices, with more than half (53%) relying on social media for news updates.[5] The internet shapes every facet of our existence, profoundly influencing how we interact with each other, consume media, and even manage our finances.

The Internet's Impact on Money

This revolution in social and economic activity has caused a corresponding shift in what constitutes ideal money. The internet has broadened the boundaries of society, making it commonplace for companies to employ global workforces and for commerce to transcend national borders. This includes the exchange of goods, media consumption, and software use on an international scale. The global nature of our 21st-century economy has, therefore, heightened the importance of one principle by which different monies compete: global accessibility. Recall how earlier this book described the importance of money to be widely recognized and accepted to function effectively. Historically, because forms of money such as wampum, cowrie shells, and gold held intrinsic value, it was intuitive for them to be widely accepted in their respective eras. Today, in our globally connected economy, there is an equal need for a form of money that is universally recognized and accepted.

Despite the global reach of the internet, over 1.4 billion people remain excluded from banking services, limiting their ability to secure credit, make payments, and participate in saving and investment for long-term financial planning.[6] Most of the unbanked population resides in poorer developing economies; within the US, minorities are overrepresented among this group. Notably, more than half of this unbanked population already owns smartphones and is active online. This suggests that the current barrier to achieving universal access to financial services is not a lack of global reach, but rather stems from an outdated financial system. This existing system, designed in the 20th century, does not adequately meet the demands of a modern, digitally connected world.

By contrast, the decline in America's use of cash today exemplifies how ingrained the economy is within the digital world. Back in the 1980s, paying with cash or check was the norm—even paying with credit cards, which first emerged in the 1950s, required a physical visit to the bank to make monthly payments. Today, by comparison, the ubiquity of smartphones obviates the need for cash entirely. A total of 41% of Americans in 2022 reported never using cash in a typical week of purchases, signifying the abundance of digital payment options available today.[7] The digital nature of our 21st-century economy has also introduced a new quality by which monies must be evaluated: digital nativeness.

A digitally native technology is one built to take full advantage of modern-day software and internet capabilities. Take the example of the common wristwatch. Initially, when "digital" watches were made, they shared the same functionality as analog watches, with the only difference being a digital display instead of a physical one. These were not "digitally native" because they simply mirrored what could already be done physically. By contrast, today's digital watches, such as the Apple watch, are digitally native because they introduce unique features only made possible by the internet: health tracking, GPS connectivity, music controls, messaging, and more. The designers of these watches thought from first principles to re-imagine what is possible in a watch fully connected to the web.

When thinking about what digitally native money comprises, two powerful features reveal themselves: sending money instantly and saving money in a digital wallet without requiring a bank or third party to store the funds. This is akin to storing gold at home instead of in a bank vault.

Because many transactions occur online today, money has the veneer of being digitally native. For example, an estimated 90% of US dollars now exists only as digital entries, manipulated through electronic systems primarily under the control of the Federal Reserve.[8] This allows for rapid adjustments in the monetary supply, with digital dollars created or eliminated in a keystroke. However, the US dollar was designed before the internet, leading to various operational challenges in adapting to a digital-dominant format.

The issues first arise whenever a bank transfer is initiated, as bank customers typically see the message:

"This payment will arrive in one to three business days." This delay directly results from the continued reliance on an antiquated "Fedwire" payment system run by the Federal Reserve that still requires hours, sometimes days, to process payment requests. Fedwire is only open during business hours, preventing individuals, businesses, and banks from conducting financial transfers at night, over the weekends, or during federally recognized holidays. A digitally native form of currency would be able to operate 24/7, 365 days a year.

Venmo, PayPal, and Cash App are widely used payment apps that allow individuals to send money instantaneously. While these applications are great for sending money between peers, they still rely on the antiquated payment systems run by the Federal Reserve to let users add and remove funds from the app. Anytime a user needs to add or withdraw funds, they must wait one to three business days for the Federal Reserve payment system to process the request. In a truly digitally native payment system, users would be able to add and withdraw funds instantaneously. In reality, users are still compelled to wait for funds to arrive. Thus, while these payment apps make the experience of interacting with a bank more intuitive, the Federal Reserve payment system constrains their functionality and speed.

The experience is even worse for anyone wishing to send international payments from their bank. The United States maintains the SWIFT network to facilitate cross-border payments that rely on a series of intermediary banks to transfer money worldwide. Due to the reliance on this complex system, these transactions often suffer from delays and inflated costs. While tech companies such as Wise (formerly known as TransferWise) are trying to improve the international payment experience, their services are still a long shot from what the world has come to expect from 21st-century software.

In this context, while it is now clear that optimal money in the 21st century is digital, the current state of the US dollar does not fully embody this ideal. Instead, what exists today is primarily an electronic representation of traditional money, managed within centralized ledgers by central and commercial banks. This arrangement signifies a transitional phase, wherein the digital potential of currency is recognized but not yet fully realized in a manner that aligns with the demands and capabilities of the modern, interconnected world.

Just as the telegraph introduced the variable of speed to money, preventing the use of gold, the internet introduced global accessibility and digital nativeness as necessities for ideal money. In other words, faster payments facilitated by the telegraph reduced gold's legitimacy as the world's reserve asset. Similarly, the proliferation of the internet suggests the world will never return to commodity money.

Modern society is now confronted with a dilemma regarding the nature of money. Traditionally, the value of money was underpinned by intrinsic properties and natural scarcity. However, the digital era introduces a paradigm where the principles governing money diverge significantly from these natural laws. Digital US dollars, unlike commodity monies of the past, are typically unconstrained by the natural scarcity of materials. Instead, they exist in a realm where supply can be expanded or contracted with relative ease, controlled by human-made systems and policies rather than the limitations of the physical world.

In essence, the transition to digital dollars represents a move away from natural scarcity toward a system where these attributes are determined by human governance. This evolution fundamentally alters the meaning of ideal money, requiring a revisit of the idea of trust discussed in Part 1.

Rearchitecting Trust

Recalling its initial emergence within hunter-gatherer societies, money evolved to solve a fundamental problem of trust. Hunter-gatherers no longer needed to trust members of foreign tribes to conduct trade; rather, they simply needed to place trust in cowrie shells as a medium of exchange. Thus, money is fundamentally a system of trust, having evolved to solve the basic problems of commerce and wealth preservation. Regarding trade, money does not *remove* trust but rather *redirects* it, such that humans place trust in the system of money rather than humans themselves. This system proved to be highly effective in fostering commercial cooperation on a large scale, but began to lose its efficacy when the underlying properties of money fell apart, eroding trust in the system itself.

The advent of the internet presents a significant challenge to traditional forms of money, especially in an era where the attributes of speed, universal accessibility, and digital compatibility are paramount. Since the dawn of the modern monetary system in 1971, the world has relied purely on human governance to manage its money. In this system, the only constraint on the scarcity of the US dollar is the discretion of the Federal Reserve and the US Treasury. Historical patterns suggest governments invariably opt to devalue or debase their currency when faced with crises or wars, viewing it as a preferable political strategy over alternatives, such as raising taxes, cutting costs, or implementing new policies. This trend is evident throughout history, from the Ancient Romans debasing the aureus for military expansion to the Dutch Empire devaluing the guilder under the strain of soaring debt. This is also occurring today, with the US government resorting to money printing to remedy issues such as the 2008 financial crisis and the 2020 COVID-19 pandemic. This recurrent theme raises an important question: Why is government devaluation of money such a frequent phenomenon despite the long-term consequences?

As Charlie Munger once famously said, "Show me the incentive, and I'll show you the outcome."[9] In this case, the incentive structures of democratic governments provide the answer. Within the US government, Congress is responsible for passing laws related to the federal government's finances. Specifically, both the House of Representatives and the Senate have budget committees responsible for constructing the federal government's yearly budget. Additionally, the Committee on Ways and Means in the House of Representatives maintains the federal government's tax code. Members of the House and

Senate who comprise these committees are subject to two- and six-year election cycles, respectively, and thus are subject to the incentives that these re-election cycles pose on their policy-making. When given the option to raise taxes, make budget cuts, or take on debt to solve a crisis or implement a new policy measure, these representatives are incentivized to choose indebtedness because raising taxes or performing budget cuts are unpopular in the eyes of their voting base. Because these candidates almost always run for re-election, they tend to favor policy decisions that are optimized for short-term wins to position themselves for the next election cycle.

Some policymakers understand the negative implications of money printing and are determined to remain fiscally responsible, even in the face of unpopularity among voters. These policymakers typically fail to remain in government for long due to the incentives of election cycles. As 20th-century economist Friedrich Hayek describes in his book *The Road to Serfdom*, politicians who persist across election cycles are the ones willing to leverage the power of political tools for short-term wins.[10] In the case of debt, representatives advocating for fiscal responsibility eventually get replaced by candidates who run campaigns promising further spending and tax cuts because these policies are more salient to the voting base.

This dynamic is best exemplified by the frequent increases made to our federal government's debt ceiling, which the US Department of the Treasury defines as:

> [T]he total amount of money that the United States government is authorized to borrow to meet its existing legal obligations, including Social Security and Medicare benefits, military salaries, interest on the national debt, tax refunds, and other payments.[11]

Raising the debt ceiling enables the US government to meet its pre-existing financial commitments resulting from decisions made by previous representatives. Whenever the government's debt approaches this arbitrary ceiling, any failure to increase this limit would lead to a catastrophic economic collapse, as it would force the government to default on its essential obligations. While there is an alternative—raising taxes or reducing spending on essential government programs—such measures never happen in practice because they ruin the reputation of politicians in the eyes of voters. Consequently, since 1960, Congress has raised the debt limit 78 times through measures that include permanent increases, temporary extensions, or redefinitions of the debt ceiling itself.

The prevailing dynamics in Congress, shaped by these existing incentives, often compel even the most well-intentioned and economically savvy members to prioritize short-term financial outcomes. These dynamics adversely affect the long-term stability of the US dollar. Those who resist this trend and advocate for longer-term economic prudence find themselves at a disadvantage, at risk of losing their positions to candidates more inclined to make such short-term concessions.

For a currency to maintain its value over the long term, its issuers must safeguard it against devaluation. This requires a design that renders it incorruptible not only to the actions of morally compromised or self-serving policymakers but, crucially, to well-intentioned politicians who must contend with the incentives of government election cycles. These cycles often drive even the most principled politicians to favor short-term legislative solutions, which can undermine the currency's stability. A truly robust monetary system requires an incorruptible structure resistant to such short-term political influences.

With the replacement of commodity money by today's government-issued fiat money, transparency arose as another key factor defining money's efficacy as a system of trust. In the past, when gold coins were in circulation or gold reserves backed paper currency, the financial system was much simpler, making it trivial for most to understand the basics of the monetary system and verify the intrinsic value of their money. There was no need for a committee to meet behind closed doors and discuss monetary policy, nor for complex financial instruments to manipulate its distribution. While there were debt-driven business cycles, the economy was self-correcting, and the vast majority of the time, one had high confidence in their ability to redeem a dollar bill for gold. Transparency was not a requirement for money because money was simple.

In the current financial landscape, where the Federal Reserve Board of Governors regulates the US dollar through a sophisticated array of financial instruments, comprehending the system poses a challenge not only to the average American but even to economists and bankers. The Federal Reserve Board, responsible for determining the US dollar's supply, consists of unelected representatives appointed by the president and confirmed by the Senate. Consequently, they do not represent the public will and operate with a degree of insulation from public scrutiny. Moreover, many of their deliberations concerning the US dollar's trajectory are conducted behind closed doors, further distancing their decision-making process from public view and understanding.

In turn, the complexity of the system overseen by the Federal Reserve Board is such that even its members struggle to make accurate economic predictions despite their expertise. This was evident when former Federal Reserve Chairwoman Janet Yellen optimistically declared in 2017:

> Will I say there will never, ever be another financial crisis? No, probably that would be going too far. I do think we're much safer and I hope that it will not [happen] in our lifetimes and I don't believe it will.[12]

This prediction was proven wrong just three years later when global financial markets faced a crisis due to the effects of the COVID-19 pandemic, requiring unprecedented central bank intervention[13] to the tune of $625 billion per week at its peak. Hardly anyone, let alone central bankers, could have predicted the extent to which COVID-19 affected the global economy, which highlights the futility of any attempts at predicting its future. In a July 2021 press conference, Federal Reserve Chairman Jerome Powell anticipated that the rise in prices experienced in the wake of

COVID-19 would be "transitory" as "inflation is expected to drop."[14] Contrary to this expectation, inflation continued to climb for the next 12 months and continues to exceed the Fed's 2% target as of this writing.

Janet Yellen, Jerome Powell, and their predecessors at the Federal Reserve are among the most astute economic minds of our era, dedicating decades to the study of macroeconomics and the global financial system. That these experts cannot make accurate forecasts about basic monetary phenomena is not a reflection of their capabilities, but rather an indictment of the complexity and unpredictability of the system itself.

Thus, in the realm of modern money, transparency into the monetary system is needed to garner society's trust. The Federal Reserve's undemocratic appointment process for its members, coupled with the lack of clear communication regarding their decision-making, obscures the actions of those shaping the dollar's monetary policy. Additionally, the intricacy of the financial structure built upon the US dollar is such that the Federal Reserve struggles to fully comprehend it, leaving the inner mechanics of the dollar system shrouded in mystery. This pervasive opacity gradually undermines trust in the dollar, eroding its long-term viability.

Additionally, the lack of transparency in the monetary system significantly hampers our ability to forecast the future value of the US dollar. In contrast to the pre-modern era, where the value of commodity-backed currencies was relatively stable and easy to predict, the US dollar's supply is not anchored to any physical commodity. Instead, it is largely influenced by the monetary policy decisions of the Federal Reserve Board of Governors. These policies, showcased during the eight annual Federal Open Market Committee (FOMC) meetings, play a pivotal role in shaping the future trajectory of the US dollar and, by extension, the US economy.

In the financial sector, each FOMC meeting is met with immense speculation and scrutiny, as the decisions made by these unelected officials have profound impacts. Before the Fed's meeting in November 2023, Wall Street bet historic sums on the event's outcome, with derivatives contracts amounting to $3 trillion in notional value based on specific policy decisions.[15] The debates and controversies that surround these meetings underscore the system's unpredictability. When seasoned Wall Street professionals struggle to anticipate the outcomes of FOMC meetings and members of the

Federal Reserve Board cannot accurately predict key economic trends, it erodes trust in the system. This unpredictability, stemming from a lack of transparent decision-making, fundamentally challenges the reliability and stability of the US monetary system.

With the rise of coin and paper currencies, the creation of money has been closely linked with government institutions, rooted in the principle that money as a system of trust requires management by an entity capable of securing the confidence of its users. In autocratic regimes, the use of money was historically enforced through coercive power. By contrast, in modern democracies, the issuance of money relies on the trust placed in the government by its citizens. In either case, governments have been the sole entities capable of garnering widespread trust and acceptance for a monetary system because of the absence of a feasible alternative. Failures in today's money, specifically the lack of scarcity, incorruptibility, transparency, and predictability, draw into question the assumption that only governments should issue currency (see the chart below for an update of the properties of money in the age of the internet). Fortunately, with the rise of the internet and advances in cryptography, a new system of trust has emerged that better meets the requirements of today's digitally native world, providing the world's first viable alternative to government-issued money.

The Properties of Money in the Age of the Internet

	Portability	Durability	Divisibility	Global Accessibility	Verifiability	Uniformity	Scarcity	Speed	Incorruptibility	Digital Nativity	Transparency	Predictability
Cowrie Shell	×	×	×	×	×							
Wampum	×	×	×	×	×							
Tobacco	×	×	×	×								
Gold	×	×	×	×	×	×	×					
Gold Backed Paper Currency	×	×	×	×	×	×	×	×				
Fiat Currency	×	×	×	×	×	×		×				

CHAPTER 8

THE BITCOIN STANDARD

Envision a type of metal that serves as a form of money—scarcer than gold, but with a dull gray color. It lacks the practical or ornamental appeal of gold and has no industrial uses. However, this metal possesses a unique and almost magical attribute: It can be transmitted to any location on the planet in an instant.

Such was the thought experiment presented to an online forum in August 2010. The "boring gray metal" was an analogy for Bitcoin, a groundbreaking digital money that embodied these unique qualities. Introduced in 2008, Bitcoin offers a solution to the money dilemma posed by the digital age: the need for digital money whose scarcity is governed by mechanisms immune to human manipulation. Through the combination of distributed networks, cryptography, and natural incentives, Bitcoin introduces a novel system of trust.

The Bitcoin network is the world's first rules-based monetary system that enables the sending, receiving, and storing of its digitally-native currency, bitcoin,* without using a central authority. Anyone with an internet connection is free to use the Bitcoin network, for it can be accessed from a personal computer, cell phone, specialized hardware "wallet," or third-party web service (e.g., Coinbase). The network is operational 24 hours a day, year-round, representing a significant improvement over the Federal Reserve's payment systems, which restrict use to business hours.

The creator of Bitcoin and the author of the "boring gray metal" forum post is Satoshi Nakamoto, a pseudonymous figure whose identity remains unknown. The mystery of Satoshi's identity was a deliberate choice, reinforcing Bitcoin's incorruptible nature. While Satoshi was initially involved in Bitcoin's development after it launched in 2009, they completely disappeared from public engagement by 2011, ensuring the network's power remains widely distributed rather than centralized under the control of any single entity.

Bitcoin is a decentralized network whose participants collectively process transactions and manage its security. Just as the ARPANET's decentralization was originally developed to reduce the

---

* Uppercase Bitcoin refers to the entire monetary system, while lowercase bitcoin refers to the currency controlled by the system.

risk of a nuclear attack bringing down the entire network, Bitcoin's decentralization gives it unprecedented security and durability. No individual or institution can unilaterally control the network or its users; failures of individual participants in the network do not compromise its integrity. Over the past decade, the network hasn't had a single delay or failure, boasting 100% uptime. Over the same period, Fedwire, one of the nation's main payment rails run by the Federal Reserve, has had numerous shutdowns, including an outage in February 2021. A system that usually transfers more than $3 trillion daily being compromised for several hours represents a threat to critical national services and is illustrative of our outdated system.[1]

Unlike the current monetary system built on the US dollar, whose rules are opaque and exceedingly complex, the Bitcoin network is run by software that is freely accessible to anyone. The rules defining the network's operation are clearly defined by code, giving complete transparency to how the system works. A key part of this codebase specifies that there will only ever be 21 million bitcoin in existence, where each bitcoin is sub-divisible into 100 million individual units called satoshis (sats for short), giving bitcoin exceptional scarcity and divisibility.

To manage the accounts of every user, the Bitcoin network maintains a ledger—a historical record of transactions. The participants of the Bitcoin network collectively store and maintain this ledger, preventing any single central authority from gaining a controlling interest—this makes the Bitcoin network "decentralized." Even though every network participant can access the network's transaction history, users remain pseudonymous, meaning their real-life identity is not tied to the account. Participants can, therefore, have full visibility of the network without violating the privacy of individuals. The transactions in the Bitcoin ledger are sent every 10 minutes in batches of transactions called "blocks," with the entire historical record of these blocks known as the "blockchain." This decentralized system ensures transparency, allowing visibility into the entire history of transactions across the network.

Access to the Bitcoin network's full codebase and transaction history enables every user to authenticate the integrity of the network. Bitcoin's software equips users with verification tools that facilitate swift and reliable authentication of network integrity. This includes verifying the owners of all bitcoin in circulation, ensuring that the rules defined in Bitcoin's codebase are followed, and verifying that individuals spend only the bitcoin they own.

This ability to perform transaction and network validation is critical to Bitcoin's overall stability and security. Bitcoin is a revolutionary system of trust insofar as it minimizes the reliance one must place on the system. Instead of needing to trust the network fully, users are empowered with the means to independently confirm that the network is functioning as expected.

The Bitcoin network functions via a robust system of checks and balances, harnessing the collective capability of its users to authenticate network activities. Although anyone can initiate a transaction, each transaction must abide by the network's rules to receive validation from a majority of network participants. This process of determining the validity of transactions is known as "consensus," acting as a safeguard against malicious or fraudulent activities, such as counterfeiting or double-spending the same bitcoin. Transactions that violate Bitcoin's established rules are immediately rejected by the network's participants.

Open access to the Bitcoin codebase allows anyone to propose network enhancements. However, these proposals must garner widespread acceptance from network participants to be implemented. This process is analogous to the amendment process of the US Constitution; amendments are rare and face stringent approval criteria. Similarly, updates to the Bitcoin network are infrequent and undergo rigorous scrutiny, prioritizing network stability and security.

Participants in the Bitcoin network are economically motivated to preserve its integrity. A network breach, if successful, would devalue bitcoin's price, rendering any stolen funds worthless. This economic incentive, combined with the network's robust checks and balances, has contributed to Bitcoin's impressive track record. Over the past decade, the network has not experienced any failures or successful hacking incidents, underscoring its resilience and security.

Monies of the past and present evolved in a path-dependent manner, subject to the immediate needs and demands of their respective societies. Bitcoin marks the first time in history that money was intentionally designed to foster a monetary system that benefits and favors the fair treatment of all actors. Recall the vital properties that have made money effective over millennia; Bitcoin was thoughtfully designed with these properties in mind:

- Because anyone with an internet connection can access and use Bitcoin, it is both **portable** and **globally accessible**.
- Because everyone can read the entire rule set and transaction history of the Bitcoin network, it is the world's most **transparent** monetary system.
- Because the network is transparent, anyone can verify the authenticity of transactions and the rule set itself, making bitcoin more **verifiable** than any previous money.
- Because of Bitcoin's decentralized design and system of checks and balances, no individual human or institution can unilaterally change the rule set or arbitrate participation in the network, making it less **corruptible** than any centrally issued money.
- Because Bitcoin's code defines a supply cap of 21 million and is incorruptible by individual actors, bitcoin is **more scarce** than any previous form of money.
- Bitcoin's defined scarcity and transparency together make it inherently **predictable** in a way that has never before been possible.

- Because the Bitcoin network is decentralized, it has no single points of failure, making it an exceptionally **durable** monetary system.
- Lastly, because each bitcoin is identical and separable into 100 million sats, it is both **uniform** and **divisible**.

Bitcoin Satisfies the Properties of 21st-Century Money

	Portability	Durability	Divisibility	Global Accessibility	Verifiability	Uniformity	Scarcity	Speed	Incorruptibility	Digital Nativity	Transparency	Predictability
Cowrie Shell	×	×	×	×	×							
Wampum	×	×	×	×	×							
Tobacco	×	×	×	×								
Gold	×	×	×	×	×	×	×					
Gold Backed Paper Currency	×	×	×	×	×	×	×	×				
Fiat Currency	×	×	×	×	×	×		×				
Bitcoin	×	×	×	×	×	×	×	×	×	×	×	×

History has shown how money can fail society in a variety of ways; Bitcoin is the product of these learnings, creating a novel system of trust that is built exclusively to satisfy money's purpose: to facilitate human flourishing by enabling societal cooperation and wealth preservation.

Bitcoin Adoption

> A mysterious new technology emerges, seemingly out of nowhere, but actually the result of two decades of intense research... Political idealists project visions of liberation and revolution onto it; establishment elites heap contempt and scorn on it. On the other hand, technologists – nerds – are transfixed by it. They see within it enormous potential and spend their nights and weekends tinkering with it. Eventually mainstream products, companies and industries emerge to commercialize it; its effects become profound; and later, many people wonder why its powerful promise wasn't more obvious from the start.[2] - Marc Andreessen

Andreessen, who created the first web browser in 1993 and later became a notable venture capitalist, describes the adoption journeys of the internet, personal computers, and Bitcoin in this quote. Such technologies typically experience a predictable growth pattern: slow initial growth followed by a rapid, almost sudden expansion before stabilizing as they become integrated into society. This pattern, resembling the shape of the letter "S" because of its "gradual then sudden" nature, is challenging for people to forecast due to its exponential nature. However, studying the rise of the internet reveals insights into this recurrent growth pattern exhibited by many technologies, including Bitcoin.

Transformative technologies and startups often originate to address a specific problem for a limited audience. Recalling the case of the internet, it was originally developed to meet the military's need for a resilient communication system that could withstand nuclear strikes. For many years following the initial development of the ARPANET, its use was limited to the US military and research scientists. To draw from a more recent example, Facebook began as a platform to connect students at Harvard University, only expanding its user base and functionality much later. In these early years of the adoption curve, groundbreaking technologies remain relatively unknown as their initial set of users is typically difficult to acquire.

When technologies successfully address an initial target problem, growth often progresses gradually, attracting people with similar needs as early adopters. For instance, after its inception in 1969, ARPANET, initially designed for military and research communication, slowly extended its network. By 1973, it had connected roughly 30 research facilities and military installations. Similarly, Facebook, which started as a platform for Harvard students, broadened its scope after its initial success. It expanded to include anyone with a student email, thereby reaching a broader but still related audience. This phase of expansion reflects a cautious yet steady approach to growing the user base while maintaining relevance to the core needs of its initial audience.

For technologies to reach the pivotal "escape velocity" characteristic of S-curve adoption, significant breakthroughs are needed to unlock the technology for the general public. In the case of the internet, this first required the development of several key technologies to improve its accessibility for the masses, such as easy access to a computer. Initially, the size and cost of computers were barriers for the casual user. The emergence of personal computers in the 1970s changed this, though initially they were primarily used for rudimentary video games, basic programming, and word processing. The real transformation came with two key developments: the creation of HTML in 1989, which simplified website creation, and Marc Andreessen's invention of the first web browser in 1993, which made internet browsing easy for the first time. These innovations made it feasible for the average personal computer user to explore the internet in a manner similar to today.

However, despite this boost in accessibility, there was a hesitancy to develop more sophisticated web pages, particularly those enabling user-generated content like basic chat forums. This reluctance stemmed from concerns about legal liability for content posted by others on their platforms. Given this new and uncharted legal territory, web developers lacked legal clarity on how such cases would be handled in court. In 1996, Congress addressed this uncertainty by passing the Communications Decency Act, aiming to provide clear regulatory guidelines for internet-related activities. A key provision of this act, Section 230, states:

> [N]o provider or user of an interactive computer service shall be treated as the publisher or speaker of any information

provided by another information content provider.[3]

The passage of this act, especially the stipulations of Section 230, significantly boosted companies' willingness to innovate on the internet, as they now understood the legal boundaries of their responsibilities. In general, paradigm-shifting technologies must often surpass these legal hurdles before breaking out into widespread adoption.

Network technologies, such as the internet or Facebook, are also subject to a phenomenon known as the "network effect." This principle suggests that a network's value grows exponentially with the addition of each new user. At first, when the network has only a few members, its value is relatively low. As the size of the network reaches a critical mass, its growth becomes self-reinforcing as the value of the network skyrockets. Consider Facebook as an example. Joining Facebook when it had just a few hundred users would be rather unappealing, given the low likelihood of finding one's friends and family on the platform. As more people joined, the number of potential connections increased, enhancing Facebook's value by increasing the chances of connecting with known contacts or creating entirely new friendships. This principle holds true for the internet and all network-based technologies: Their value depends on user participation. Once a critical mass of users is reached, a significant spike in value follows, fueling the explosive growth characteristic of the "S-curve" adoption pattern.

Finally, for groundbreaking technologies to achieve widespread adoption, they must earn user trust. Gaining this trust can be challenging in the early and middle stages of a technology's lifecycle, particularly when established experts who have built their careers on previous paradigms critique the new technology. The internet in its early years faced a slew of disparaging criticisms, including a remark from Nobel laureate economist Paul Krugman in 1998, "By 2005 or so, it will become clear that the Internet's impact on the economy has been no greater than the fax machine's."[4] While it's easy to dismiss such a statement today, at the time, many shared this skepticism as the world was on the precipice of the internet revolution. Trust is arguably the most challenging attribute for a technology to acquire, as it often requires the simple passage of time to demonstrate viability.

Thus, for the internet to finally break out in 1998, four conditions were needed:

1) Improved user accessibility to allow anyone to browse the web easily.

2) Regulatory clarity to give companies the go-ahead to innovate in the space.

3) Enough users for a network effect to provide sufficient value to the network.

4) Time for the public to build trust in its viability and effectiveness.

With the confluence of these four phenomena, the internet entered the hyper-growth stage of its S-curve adoption, and by the mid-2000s, it had gone mainstream.

As shown in the accompanying graph, the S-curve adoption pattern is not exclusive to the internet but is a typical trajectory for transformative technologies. It provides a useful framework for assessing the current stage of a technology's growth. Bitcoin's adoption curve follows a similar path. As a decentralized network akin to the internet, four key conditions must be met for Bitcoin to gain widespread global adoption:

1) It must be intuitively accessible to the average person.

2) It needs regulatory clarity from the government.

3) It needs enough users to build a proper network effect.

4) Most importantly, it must garner enough trust to overcome previous apprehensions.

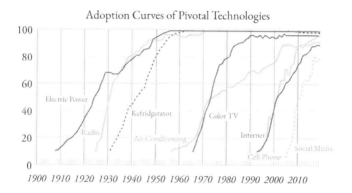

The adoption curves of many impactful technologies.[5]

Understanding Bitcoin's current position on the S-curve and which of the four necessary properties it satisfies requires a brief review of its history. Initially, Bitcoin was regarded as an intriguing experiment within a niche community of cypherpunks, libertarians, and dark-web enthusiasts. This group, active in specialized online forums, had been exploring cryptography and digital currency for years. Before Bitcoin, various decentralized digital currencies had been proposed in these circles, including "Hashcash" in 1997 and "b-money" in 1998.[6] Key ideas from these early digital currency concepts significantly influenced

Bitcoin's design. When Satoshi Nakamoto first introduced Bitcoin, it was seen merely as another project aligning with the ongoing research of cypherpunks and cryptographers, unlikely to break into the mainstream. Over time, however, Bitcoin evolved beyond its theoretical roots, gradually gaining recognition and acceptance as a legitimate form of digital currency.

A notable early transaction in Bitcoin's history occurred in May 2010, when a programmer traded 10,000 bitcoin for two pizzas, facilitated by another forum user who arranged for the delivery from Papa Johns. This exchange, which at today's value represents a substantial sum, highlights Bitcoin's niche and experimental beginnings.

By 2013, its usage had expanded beyond these initial niche groups to various small communities worldwide. These communities, often marginalized from traditional financial systems due to lack of banking access, sanctions, or discrimination, began adopting Bitcoin for their financial transactions. One notable story of such grassroots Bitcoin adoption is that of female Afghan entrepreneur Roya Mahboob.

Roya Mahboob established the Afghan Citadel Software Company (ACSC) in 2010, a forward-thinking initiative to integrate women into

Afghanistan's emerging tech sector. This strategic initiative recognized the nascent state of technology in Afghanistan and sought to involve women from the outset.[7] However, Roya's path was fraught with obstacles; beyond facing threats and backlash from the Taliban, she confronted the challenge of compensating her female employees. Traditional payment methods, such as cash, proved unfeasible as women often had their earnings confiscated by family members, and societal norms barred many women from owning bank accounts. In other words, the existing forms of money at the time were not serving her needs.

The turning point came in 2013 when Mahboob discovered Bitcoin. It not only facilitated financial transactions, but also granted women newfound financial autonomy. Bitcoin's unique features, particularly its storage and transaction capabilities, reduced the risk of physical confiscation or male family interference. Bitcoin's ability to be securely kept on compact devices no larger than a flash drive allowed Afghan women to control their finances independently.

Alex Gladstein of the Human Rights Foundation has written extensively about the transformative impact of Bitcoin in his book *Check Your Financial Privilege*. One such story highlights one of Roya Mahboob's employees. Forced to flee Afghanistan because of a threat to her life, she traveled through Iran and Turkey, eventually making it to Germany. Along the way, she brought her life savings, stored as bitcoin. Upon arrival in Germany, she converted her saved bitcoin into euros, allowing her to start a new life.[8] Before Bitcoin, she would have had to flee while leaving all of her life savings behind.

The stories of Roya Mahboob and her employees are some of the many cases of grassroots Bitcoin adoption seen throughout its history and are emblematic of Bitcoin's early growth following the classic S-curve model. In late 2012, Coinbase, a major crypto exchange, first launched, allowing users to buy, sell, and store bitcoin easily. Hardware wallets, devices the size of a flash drive that enable users to store their bitcoin without needing a computer or phone, also entered the market around this time. Together, these innovations were a substantial improvement over alternatives at the time and were crucial steps in unlocking accessibility for the masses. By 2014, Bitcoin's user base had expanded into the millions, propelled by the advent of mobile applications that simplified bitcoin transactions.

Around this time, Bitcoin surpassed serving as merely an alternative form of money—in Venezuela, it had become the money of choice. Venezuela was once considered the shining economy of Latin America, blessed with oil riches and the highest per capita income in the region. However, fiscal mismanagement and a decline in oil prices left the country vulnerable.[9] When Nicolás Maduro took power in 2012, he expanded the already large national debt, implementing populist policies such as free gasoline and extensive government food programs. These measures, aimed at short-term gains, eventually led to the devaluation of the bolivar (Venezuela's official currency) to manage the soaring debt. Maduro's authoritarian measures compounded this economic decline, including internet restrictions and the persecution of political opponents.[10] Venezuela officially entered hyperinflation in 2017, with prices of goods doubling every six weeks. The hyperinflation peaked in 2018, reaching an annual rate of 63,000%, and has remained exceedingly high ever since.[11]

The hopelessness of using the bolivar for saving or even transacting compelled Venezuelans to turn to other forms of money to fulfill these needs. The US dollar emerged as a preferred medium of exchange, used in black-market economies due to its widespread acceptance and stability in value. However, escalating sanctions from the United States throughout the Bush,

Obama, and Trump administrations rendered the dollar unfeasible for remittances—the act of loved ones abroad sending money back home for support—which are relied on by nearly 30% of the Venezuelan population.[12] Thus, Bitcoin emerged as a reliable way for Venezuelans to receive remittances due to its universal accessibility around the globe.

Through this process, Venezuelans turned to Bitcoin as one of the few viable ways of preserving wealth. Andrea O'Sullivan from the James Madison Institute elaborates:

> People living in Venezuela are living under a very unstable and predatory government. They suffer from extreme inflation and general economic instability. And here's a censorship-resistant, inflation-proof asset, so [Bitcoin is] very attractive to people who are looking for a way to maintain value.[13]

Since 2014, over seven million Venezuelans have fled their homeland to seek refuge status elsewhere.[10] The process of fleeing Venezuela to a new country is not without risk, making it difficult to bring many belongings along the way. As such, Bitcoin became widely used as a way to preserve savings while finding a new home: A refugee can convert their savings to bitcoin, which is then stored on a small device and kept with them until they arrive at their destination, where the bitcoin can then be converted to the local currency.

While Venezuela is an extreme case, it represents Bitcoin's rapid international adoption since 2014. By contrast, Western institutions were initially hesitant to become involved in the space due to a lack of clarity on how the courts would litigate Bitcoin. This began to change in 2015 when the Commodity Futures Trading Commission (CFTC), an independent US government agency responsible for regulating US derivatives markets, announced that it would classify Bitcoin as a commodity. This placed Bitcoin alongside the likes of gold and oil in the Commodity Exchange Act, giving US corporations the clarity they needed to understand how Bitcoin would be taxed and what legal restrictions were placed on its usage. Since then, a host of additional policy measures have been passed within the US and internationally, giving the global financial community confidence to become involved in the space. As a result, Bitcoin has garnered recognition within the broader investment community, finding its place in millions of retirement accounts, pension funds, university endowments, sovereign wealth funds, asset management firms, and actively managed hedge funds.

With this additional regulatory clarity, Bitcoin's network effect has rapidly grown, with roughly 300 million people globally using bitcoin for transactions or as a wealth-preservation tool today. In 2023, the number of merchants accepting bitcoin as payment surged by 174%.[14] According to the latest data, the total value of circulating bitcoin ranks it among the top 20 global currencies, comparable to the Swiss france and the Australian dollar. In sub-Saharan Africa, Bitcoin accounts for almost 10% of regional transaction volume, as grassroots adoption in Ghana, Kenya, and Nigeria has accelerated in recent years.[15] El Salvador has even adopted Bitcoin as legal tender, integrating it into their economies and national reserves. In fact, Bitcoin is rapidly replacing gold as the preferred inflation-resistant store-of-value asset, representing 10% of the total value of all the gold ever mined.

Recently, the introduction of bitcoin-based exchange-traded funds (ETFs) opened avenues for Americans to easily access bitcoin through their existing retirement accounts. It also allows for bitcoin's inclusion in mutual funds and investment strategies recommended by financial advisers. As many as 77% of financial advisers are now recommending a bitcoin ETF product to their clientele.[16] Notably, some of the world's largest and most respected asset management firms, including Blackrock, Fidelity, and Invesco, offer these bitcoin-focused investment products. With their involvement in bitcoin products, these prominent Wall Street institutions are now motivated to actively promote bitcoin as a viable asset class. This includes marketing efforts directed at their clientele and advocacy and lobbying efforts in Washington to support the wider adoption and regulatory acceptance of Bitcoin. While it is hard to pinpoint exactly when a technology has gained the critical mass of trust needed to expand rapidly, Wall Street's endorsement is an objective signpost—those at the top of traditional finance are beginning to understand and trust the Bitcoin network.

As of this writing, Bitcoin's stage in its adoption curve is comparable to that of the internet in 2000, as illustrated in the chart below. The technology has matured to a point where it's easily accessible to the average person, and regulatory clarity has improved to the extent that major firms confidently engage in the space. Bitcoin's network effect is beginning to hit a critical mass, now being used by roughly 300 million people across the globe.[8] The growing trust in Bitcoin, underscored by its reliable 15-year track record, is prompting Wall Street to reconsider its initial reluctance to get involved. The year 2000 was when the internet exploded in usage because it had finally satisfied the four requirements necessary for hyper-adoption. Bitcoin is in a similar place today and is poised to rapidly expand to all corners of the globe.

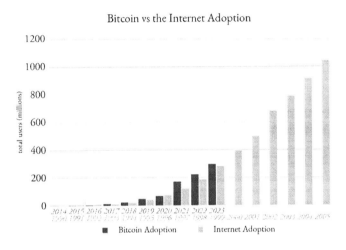

User adoption of the internet vs. Bitcoin.[17]

CHAPTER 9

DIGITAL GOLD

Blaise Pascal was a 17ᵗʰ-century polymath renowned for his contributions to mathematics, philosophy, physics, and theology. Despite his many inventions and theories, Pascal's most well-known idea was strikingly simple. First introduced in the posthumously published work *Pensées,* "Pascal's wager" suggests that it is more rational to live as if God exists. Pascal's reasoning is straightforward: If God does not exist, the believer loses little, merely abstaining from certain behaviors discouraged by the church. However, if God does exist, believing in Him offers immeasurable rewards, including eternal life and escape from eternal punishment. This simple yet compelling logic, born out of the ambiguity surrounding the existence of God, finds a modern parallel in the game theory of Bitcoin's growth. This presents a modern version of the concept, which we will call "Satoshi's wager."

With a growing user base of about 300 million and an increasing share of global wealth, Bitcoin's chances of widespread adoption are significant enough to merit attention.[1] Although there's no certainty of Bitcoin's ultimate success, its real potential to become the dominant currency of the 21st century means that there is now a rational strategy for both individuals and institutions, even those not actively using Bitcoin, to acquire a small amount as a hedge against the possibility of Bitcoin's ubiquitous acceptance in the future. While the likelihood of this happening is uncertain, the finite potential losses involved in such a hedge*[8] are more than offset by the significant rewards should bitcoin become a dominant global currency. If Bitcoin fails to achieve widespread adoption, the financial impact of this hedge is minimal. However, if bitcoin emerges as a global currency, even a small amount acquired as a hedge will have transformed into a meaningful amount of wealth.

The concept of Satoshi's wager extends beyond individuals to encompass corporations, pension funds, and nation-states. For example, central banks and sovereign wealth funds are tasked with managing their nations' surplus reserves. These reserves typically

---

* Hedging: an investment strategy where one makes an investment to offset the outcomes of possible events occurring. For example, buying a flood insurance policy is a "hedge" against the occurrence of a flood.

comprise a diverse portfolio featuring key assets like the US dollar, euro, Japanese yen, and gold. The allocation of each asset in these portfolios often reflects its prominence in the global monetary system. For instance, in 2021, the US dollar accounted for approximately 59% of foreign currency reserves held by central banks, a figure that has been gradually decreasing since 2015.[2] In the same year, bitcoin marked its entry into national reserves when El Salvador began accumulating bitcoin with its surpluses, which, as of March 2024, amounts to the equivalent of $206 million.[3] Following this, several other countries, including a sovereign wealth fund of the United Arab Emirates and the Kingdom of Bhutan,[4,5] have publicly disclosed related investments in the Bitcoin space. As Bitcoin's adoption grows, central banks and sovereign wealth funds will be increasingly incentivized to add bitcoin to their portfolios.

Insurance companies and multinational corporations are also responsible for managing substantial amounts of wealth, prioritizing value preservation over explicit profit-making. For these entities, bitcoin serves as an effective safeguard against the declining value of the US dollar. In 2020, MassMutual, a global leader in life insurance, took a strategic step by incorporating bitcoin into its investment portfolio.[6] Following suit the next year, automotive giant Tesla diversified its assets with a $1.5 billion investment in bitcoin.[7]

Savvy hedge fund investors who attempt to stay ahead of prominent macroeconomic trends have also caught on to the appeal of bitcoin. Historically, active investors would hedge against inflationary periods and government devaluation of currency by purchasing gold, which has long been known as a "safe haven" asset. Bitcoin has been replacing gold in this role, becoming the safe haven of choice for the world's largest hedge funds. Ray Dalio, who managed more than $100 billion at his hedge fund Bridgewater Associates, has been a long-time supporter of the asset, once saying, "Personally, I'd rather have a bitcoin than a bond."[8] More recently, BlackRock CEO Larry Fink, who oversees nearly $9 trillion in managed assets, said Bitcoin could "revolutionize finance."[9] Seeing these thought leaders support Bitcoin is the game theory of Satoshi's wager playing out in real time. For these institutions, it is rational to add bitcoin as a small portion of their reserves, just in case it catches on.

The growing recognition of Bitcoin as a tool for wealth preservation has prompted major financial institutions and Wall Street banks to introduce Bitcoin-related services. User-friendly apps such as

PayPal and Cash App have made Bitcoin widely accessible, while esteemed asset managers, including Fidelity and NASDAQ, now offer bitcoin custody services.

My personal experience (Sam Baker) on Wall Street provided a unique perspective. During my tenure at Citigroup, one of the world's largest banks, I was employed as part of a team focused on Bitcoin and cryptocurrency applications. What became clear to me was how Wall Street is acutely aware of the disruptive potential of new forms of money and is actively seeking ways to integrate these innovations into existing business models. While institutions such as Citigroup may publicly maintain a cautious stance toward Bitcoin given their deep roots in the traditional financial system, their behind-the-scenes actions speak volumes. Nearly every large Wall Street bank now employs a team dedicated to blockchain research, investment, and development. Such significant hiring in recent years is a testament to Wall Street's gradual yet unmistakable shift toward embracing Bitcoin and its underlying technologies.

As the number of individuals and institutions making Satoshi's wager grows, Bitcoin's network effect expands. Each time a large company, asset manager, or central bank invests in bitcoin as a strategic hedge, it signals growing confidence in Bitcoin's viability as a form of money. Each endorsement enhances Bitcoin's value and trustworthiness, further encouraging widespread adoption. Consequently, this increased confidence attracts more attention from the global community and individuals, who now view bitcoin as a credible asset. Unlike traditional currencies, whose supply often expands in response to increased value, bitcoin's supply remains fixed. Therefore, any significant growth in its perceived legitimacy and trust correlates directly with a sharp rise in its price. In this context, the game theory behind Satoshi's wager acts as a self-fulfilling prophecy: Rational decisions by individuals and institutions increasingly point to Bitcoin's ascendance as a preeminent form of global currency. As more individuals and institutions use bitcoin as money for saving and transacting, its utility grows.

Layered Money

Over its 15-year existence, bitcoin has gone from being virtually valueless to boasting a market valuation exceeding $1 trillion and has yet to experience a single impactful episode of corruption, fraud, or counterfeiting.* The emergence of a form of money from nothing is unprecedented in history; monies historically originated as commodities with existing value or were backed by such commodities before transitioning into fiat money. To understand how Bitcoin has achieved such organic success and to forecast its future trajectory, it is worth looking at some of the fundamental principles of systems engineering.

In his seminal work *Systemantics*, John Gall was the first to articulate what is now known as Gall's Law:

> A complex system that works is invariably found to have evolved from a simple system that works. The inverse proposition also appears to be true: A complex system designed from scratch never works and cannot be made to work.[10]

Gall's Law underscores the importance of simplicity in the design of scalable systems. Overcomplicating a system during its initial design phase is often a recipe for failure, as exemplified by the ambitious creation of Brazil's capital city in the mid-20th century.

---

* Readers may recall the FTX fraud case. FTX was a cryptocurrency exchange that fraudulently exploited customer funds. Notably, the Bitcoin network was not hacked or affected in any way. However, users who bought and held bitcoin on FTX's platform were. More will be discussed in the epilogue.

In 1956, President Juscelino Kubitschek de Oliveira made a promise to the Brazilian people: to relocate the nation's capital inland from the port city of Rio de Janeiro. There was a growing desire among the population to tap into the potential of Brazil's vast interior, abundant in natural resources and land. As such, President Kubitschek commissioned a plan to establish Brasilia, a modernist utopian city that would be built from scratch, deep within the northern highlands of Brazil.[11,12]

Modern-Day Brasilia.[13]

Inaugurated in 1960, Brasilia emerged from the visionary collaboration of architect Oscar Niemeyer and urban planner Lúcio Costa. Its groundbreaking design, reminiscent of an airplane or bird when viewed from above, segregated the city into specialized housing, administration, and commerce zones. However, challenges surfaced rapidly after its inauguration. The city's meticulously planned structure failed to replicate the natural development seen in older cities, resulting in problems such as socio-economic divides, transportation issues, and insufficient accommodation for lower-income residents. A notable point of criticism was the city's vast, elaborate public spaces; while visually impressive, they lacked practical utility for everyday public life. Today, while Brasilia is home to over 2.5 million people, 90% of this population resides outside the originally planned area, preferring the 27 satellite towns that emerged and expanded naturally.[14]

In contrast to Brasilia's top-down design, systems that started simple and only became complex after a long process of maturation, such as Facebook, illustrate the effectiveness of organic growth. Facebook began as a website restricted to Harvard University students. After this simple prototype demonstrated traction, Facebook founder Mark Zuckerberg opened up the website to college campuses across the US, choosing a scalable and adaptable approach to product development. Only after proving its viability within college campuses nationwide did Zuckerberg open up the platform to everyone. Facebook's newsfeed and mobile app, two features that are core to the experience today, were not introduced until two and four years after its initial launch, respectively. While it's easy to imagine that Facebook was destined for greatness from the outset, it was rather through its iterative approach to product development modeled after Gall's Law that it could rapidly adapt to the needs of a growing user base.

Similarly, gold-based monetary systems initially began in simplicity, using coins for transactions and savings. This primitive form, reliant solely on physical gold, was simple yet effective, as the tangible nature of gold coins instilled confidence in their value. However, as economies expanded and became more complex, these basic gold-coin systems evolved to accommodate growing demands.

Gold-backed paper money was introduced for gold to scale beyond this "base layer" of physical transactions. Issued by banks that stored the corresponding gold, this paper money served as a "second layer," enabling the gold monetary system to scale in both size and complexity. This second layer facilitated long-distance transactions and the provisioning of credit by financial institutions, adding certain advantages over the gold-coin system.

As gold monetary systems continued to scale and increase in complexity, paper money increasingly became the predominant form of currency. This system was successful for a long period throughout the 1800s but began to fray as technological advancements rendered gold unfit as base layer money for modern society. At this point, gold became increasingly centralized in the vaults of commercial and central banks, which held it on behalf of clients. This trend toward centralization ultimately led to the demise of the gold standard, as it allowed governments to easily assume control of gold reserves and inflate the currency supply. The fiat money system that followed was not born out of simplicity, but arose from the path-dependent development of money in the 20th century. It began as the offspring of the Bretton Woods system, designed from the top down in a complex fashion.

In contrast to the complexity of the US dollar system, bitcoin exemplifies Gall's Law. Originating from a design conceived from first principles, the base layer of Bitcoin is similar to that of physical gold. Paraphrasing author and Bitcoin advocate Allen Farrington, Bitcoin does not move fast and break things. It moves slowly and breaks nothing.[15] While Bitcoin offers an improvement upon many attributes of fiat currencies, it was not designed to replace the entire US dollar system at the outset. Instead, it was designed to prioritize monetary attributes essential for enabling widespread financial freedom and societal welfare, namely scarcity and incorruptibility.

As described in earlier chapters, money serves as a medium of exchange *and* as a store of value. Balancing these functions involves trade-offs in any currency system. Fiat currencies, such as the US dollar, are effective mediums of exchange, but have lost their effectiveness as stores of value after leaving a gold standard. Conversely, Bitcoin has been gaining prominence due to its effectiveness as a store of value because it was explicitly designed with the properties of scarcity, security, and incorruptibility. Therefore, it is likely that "base layer" Bitcoin will eventually not be used in everyday transactions as a currency, but as a primary savings device for individuals and institutions. Its role as a medium of exchange will scale over time as Bitcoin continues to mature into a more complex system. Second-layer solutions built on top of the network already exist to enhance Bitcoin's ability to process many transactions for daily commerce.

The Lightning Network is one such scaling solution that has gained popularity in recent years. It is a decentralized network built on top of the Bitcoin network that enables instantaneous, near-zero fee transactions. Unlike the Bitcoin network, the Lightning Network can process up to one million transactions per second, surpassing the processing capabilities of even Visa, which can send up to 65,000 transactions per second.[16] The development and adoption of second-layer systems like the Lightning Network make it clear that Bitcoin's slow transaction throughput will not limit its widespread adoption. Just as second- and third-layer systems emerged in the past to improve the transaction processing capabilities of gold, so too will systems be built on top of Bitcoin to support its scaling globally.

Unlike gold, Bitcoin's digital nature simplifies storage and payments, allowing for second-layer complexity that avoids the centralizing pitfalls that caused the demise of gold systems. Converting second-layer currencies backed by bitcoin to actual bitcoin will be as simple as a few clicks in an online banking interface. While such redemptions might be infrequent, this ease of conversion significantly enhances trust within the monetary system by allowing users to take self-custody of their bitcoin at any time. This ability will prevent the supply of bitcoin from centralizing into the hands of second-layer intermediaries and maintain the decentralized integrity of the system at large. Regardless of its future role in everyday transactions, Bitcoin's effectiveness as a store of value has been well-established, providing a stable foundation for monetary systems of the future.

The Downfall of the Dollar and the Rise of Bitcoin

The rise of this future monetary system, centered on a reliable store of value, is occurring in parallel with the gradual downfall of the existing dominant form of money. As such, we live in the midst of a transitionary period. On the one hand, the US dollar no longer serves the needs of society as intended and is bound to inflate over time to ease the federal government's debt burden. Neither Americans nor foreigners have reason to believe in the dollar's ability to retain value over time and, therefore, are rapidly losing trust in this monetary system. To visualize this loss of trust is as simple as examining the following chart, showing the US dollar's steady yet rapid decline in purchasing power.[17]

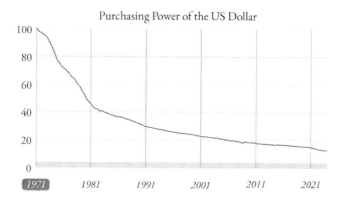

Since 2007, the purchasing power of the dollar, or the effective amount a consumer can purchase with the dollar, has consistently declined.[17]

On the other side of this transitional period, Bitcoin has emerged organically as an alternative that directly addresses what the US dollar lacks: a reliable store of value that is an open form of money built for the modern era. Throughout its existence, Bitcoin has been successful in gaining the trust of millions of people around the globe, as seen in the historical graph of bitcoin's value.[18]

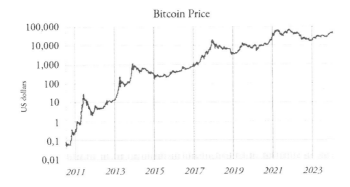

Contrasting the fall of the US dollar, the price of bitcoin has precipitously increased since its inception. Note that the y-axis has a logarithmic scale.[18]

Living in the year 2000, it was easy to see the rapid growth of the internet that occurred in the 1990s, yet it was equally difficult to project this growth forward and appreciate the implications of such change. Bitcoin is where the internet was in 2000: its adoption growing rapidly and benefit to society becoming clear, yet not entirely realized. With all the pieces in place for parabolic growth characteristic of classic S-curve adoption, the game theory of Satoshi's wager is beginning to unfold at an increasingly rapid pace. Individuals, investors, and marquee financial institutions are investing in Bitcoin because they see the promise of the technology and the potential for its growth. As Bitcoin continues to mature in the same manner as the internet, the coming decade will see its use become ubiquitous.

CHAPTER 10

THE SOVEREIGN INDIVIDUAL

While Bitcoin remains on the precipice of parabolic growth, characteristic of S-curve style adoption, it has already meaningfully impacted the lives of millions around the world. For those living in developed nations where the erosion of money is a relatively subtle phenomenon, the value of the Bitcoin network is not immediately apparent. But for those who must live with hyperinflating currencies, oppressive regimes, and corrupt financial institutions, the virtues of Bitcoin are self-evident, for these people viscerally understand the importance of reliable and incorruptible money. What follows is a detailing of several instances where Bitcoin is already transforming the lives of the oppressed. In doing so, we hope to demonstrate the profound benefits that come from an improvement in money.

Modern-Day Imperialism

In central Africa lies a group of 15 countries collectively known as the African Financial Community (CFA).

Today, 183 million people live in the CFA zone across the nations of Benin, Burkina Faso, Cameroon, Central African Republic, Chad, the Comoros, Equatorial Guinea, Gabon, Guinea-Bissau, the Ivory Coast, Mali, Niger, the Republic of Congo, Senegal, and Togo.[1] Notably, the CFA comprises many of the world's poorest nations. According to the United Nations, 11 of the 15 are classified as Least Developed Countries, and the remaining four have experienced an economic decline in recent decades.[2] According to economists Fanny Pigeaud and Ndongo Samba Sylla, authors of the book *Africa's Last Colonial Currency: The CFA Franc Story*, the purchasing power of individuals in the region has dropped precipitously over the last 40 years, with incomes also falling every year of the 21st-century.[3] This is one of the most economically impoverished regions in the world, which paradoxically resides over plentiful natural resources and is home to a large, working-age population. Given that this impoverishment is pervasive across all CFA nations, what is the root cause of such a terrible economic track record?

During the celebrations of Chad's 55th year of independence in August 2015, Chad's President Idriss Déby touched on the mechanism many Africans believe is the root cause of the CFA's economic failure.

He boldly remarked that "we must have the courage to say there is a cord preventing development in Africa that must be severed"—the "cord" he referenced is the CFA franc, a currency that has oppressed the region since its inception.[2] A decree of French General Charles de Gaulle officially created the CFA franc in December 1945 in the wake of the Bretton Woods Agreement. At the time, all CFA member states were French colonies; to foster economic unity among them, France created the CFA franc, a legally enforced monopoly of money across the region. Nevertheless, international pressure was mounting for European powers to decolonize Africa. In response, France formally moved out of the region in 1956 under legislation known as "La Loi-cadre Defferre," granting the colonies their own democratic institutions, increased autonomy, and universal suffrage. However, these colonies were significant sources of wealth, and thus, France was reluctant to cede complete control of the region to Africa, and it managed to keep the CFA franc in place. This continued hegemony over the CFA's monetary system enabled France to subtly maintain economic control of the region and simultaneously make the claim that it had granted independence back to its African colonies.[1]

The CFA franc monetary system was built around unlimited convertibility with euros, as guaranteed by the French government. With this convertibility in place, the French required that each member nation maintain 50% of their foreign exchange reserves in a French Treasury "operating account." CFA francs retain value only within their own region, as they are not accepted for payment by countries outside the CFA zone. Consequently, any international trade involving these countries must be conducted through France. To conduct trade, CFA nations must exchange francs for euros, where the French Treasury extracts a fee by giving fewer euros back than the value of the francs.[2] Additionally, France manufactures all francs used in the CFA, charging $45 million per year for their production, and holds 90% of all the gold reserves of CFA nations. Perhaps the most surprising component of the system is France's privilege of first right of refusal: Anytime a business within the CFA wants to import goods or sell services internationally, they must first make the offer to French companies before turning elsewhere.[1]

In essence, this system grants the French Treasury immense control over the region's economics, allowing France to effectively levy taxes through devaluations of the currency and exchange rate seigniorage. The magnitude of this impact is best summarized by the franc's devaluation over time. Since its inception, the exchange rate between the franc and euro has been repeatedly modified, resulting in a devaluation of the franc by 99.5% by the mid-90s.[1]

As a result of limited domestic credit through the CFA zone, the region has a small industrial base. Therefore, it must rely heavily on imported materials and products to sustain its economy. The French Treasury extracts wealth with each import by creating a favorable exchange rate between the franc and the euro. And because the region cannot bootstrap industrialization efficiently by turning to global investors, the economies are limited to producing a small set of basic commodities. As described by Ndongo Samba Sylla:

> For those hoping to export competitive products, obtain affordable credit, work for the integration of continental trade, or fight for an Africa free from imperialist control, the CFA franc is an anachronism demanding orderly and methodical elimination.[2]

Beyond preventing proper economic development, the CFA franc runs counter to the Western ideals of self-determination and self-sovereignty. Anyone who supports democratic ideals agrees that people have a right to define their own systems of governance, which extends to the right to control one's financial system. In speaking about the CFA franc, Benin President Patrice Talon said, "Psychologically, with regards to the vision of sovereignty and managing your own money, it's not good that this model continues [...]."[3] His views are widely shared by African intellectuals, bankers, and politicians. Even though France claims to have granted sovereignty to CFA nations dating back to 1956, because of its tight economic control over its monetary system, in practice, it still has an imperial grip over the area.

Many African leaders are afraid to speak out against the French, given France's long history of ousting leaders who attempted to move off the franc and create their own currency. Sylla states:

> France has never hesitated to jettison heads of state tempted to withdraw from the system. Most were removed from office or killed in favour of more compliant leaders who cling to power come hell or high water, as shown by the CAEMC nations and Togo.[2]

Pigeaud and Sylla's research supports these findings, as "Paris carried out nearly 40 military interventions in 16 countries to defend its interests."[3] For example, in 2011, the Ivory Coast attempted to create its own currency to escape the CFA franc zone under the leadership of President Laurent Gbagbo. When the Ivory Coast was in the advanced stages of implementing their new currency, France launched a military attack on the country, bombing the presidential palace, military barracks, and residence of the Ivorian head of state. The operation ended on April 11, when the French military attacked the Ivorian army and arrested President Gbagbo.[3] To this day, CFA countries like the Ivory Coast are trapped in a system that enforces economic deterioration because of France's historical pattern of maintaining the franc's hegemony with coercion and force.

At the turn of the 21st century, the advent of new technologies gave hope to Africans, with the rise of mobile phones and social media opening a new opportunity to resist the use of the franc. These platforms enabled people to organize in a decentralized manner, making it harder for officials in support of the franc to crack down on the resistance. As a result, the anti-CFA movement has gained considerable traction over the past decade.

One prominent member of the movement is Fodé Diop, an engineer, entrepreneur, and Bitcoin advocate.

Fodé is from Senegal, a CFA nation that ranks 103rd in the world in terms of economic freedom.[5] Within Senegal, saving money for the future is a foreign concept. As soon as the Senegalese earn francs, they spend them. This is not due to a lack of financial education, but rather directly results from the extreme inflation experienced by the franc since its inception. The Senegalese have no confidence in their financial system, believing that banks cannot be trusted and that the franc cannot store value into the future. According to Fodé, "[This idea] may sound crazy to Americans, but for Senegalese or Togolese, central banks are a parasite on our society."[1]

The Senegalese also lack the proper financial infrastructure to support even basic financial activities like sending money and saving it for a rainy day. Fodé says that "when you go to Senegal, more than 70% of people have never stepped foot in a bank. Mom never had a credit card or debit card."[1] Senegalese citizens do not have access to financial applications that Westerners have grown accustomed to—not even apps like Venmo, PayPal, and Cash App exist in the country.

As a result of the severe lack of financial infrastructure in the CFA combined with the economic destruction reaped by the CFA franc, Africans are increasingly turning to Bitcoin as an alternative. To them, bitcoin is not just some digital coin that they can speculate on; it instead offers the first opportunity to save money for the future without fear of government devaluation. The Senegalese, who traditionally do not have access to a bank or online financial tools, can now buy and save their wealth through the Bitcoin network. To the Senegalese, Bitcoin functions as a promising currency, bank, and payment network all wrapped up into a system they can access from their phones.

When Fodé discovered Bitcoin in 2010, he immediately recognized its potential to fight the franc's oppression by offering a way out for Africans: "When I go home, I see how people are being held down. But in the same way we leapfrogged landlines and went straight to cell phones, we're going to skip banks and go straight to Bitcoin."[1] Fodé believes that as more Africans gain access to electricity and the internet, they will opt to purchase bitcoin directly as a means to gain financial freedom.[1]

Bineta, another Senegalese entrepreneur, shares this vision with Fodé. She is the founder of Bleu Comme La Mer, a seafood marketplace connecting fishermen directly with consumers, removing the middleman. In starting her business, Bineta had the vision to streamline the fishing industry and ultimately reduce overfishing. More deeply, she recognized the potential of Bitcoin for Senegal and thus made Bleu the first business in Senegal to accept bitcoin as payment. For Bineta, Bitcoin is the money of the future for the country:

> The more I learned, the more I realized we need this. This kind of money will help overcome so many issues. Not only is Bitcoin a tool for freedom, but the technology underpinning Bitcoin such as blockchain and decentralization will change Africa's development.[6]

Entrepreneurs and business owners across the CFA zone are beginning to appreciate the power of Bitcoin in its ability to help businesses escape the franc. Gloire, the founder of a refugee project in the Congo called Kiveclair, said, "Bitcoin can help the countries of the CFA Zone to free themselves from France to finally turn the dark page of colonization."[7] To people like Gloire, Bineta, and Fodé, Bitcoin is a lifesaving technology because it provides a way for developing nations to gain economic independence and the means for individuals to finally save for the future in a predictable, reliable, and secure manner.

Cuba Monetary Oppression

The story of economic stagnation as a result of extractive monetary systems is not unique to central Africa—a similar pattern of exploitative monetary systems exists all over the globe, including in modern-day Cuba. In the 1950s, Cuba was one of the wealthiest countries in Latin America; its income per capita was greater than Spain and Portugal and even exceeded that of Mexico by 70%.[8] This all changed when Fidel Castro rose to power in 1959, setting off a series of events that would destroy the Cuban economy.

Castro implemented a communist regime throughout Cuba and quickly built political relations with the Soviet Union, a fellow communist ally. The Soviets began purchasing a majority of Cuban exports and even subsidized the country as a way of supporting the growth of communism globally. Thus, when the Soviet Union collapsed in 1991, Cuba saw roughly $5 billion in annual subsidies vanish and lost the main purchaser of its exports. The Cuban peso devalued by over 95% against the US dollar. The 1990s came to be known as the "Special Period" within Cuba, where most Cubans could only afford one meal per day and industry collapsed nationwide.[1]

As a result, Cubans needed to turn to other means to support their families and earn even a basic living.

Increasingly, Cubans fled overseas, sending remittance payments to their family members still residing in Cuba. Today, it is estimated that a total of $3 billion is sent back as remittances to Cuba annually.[9] However, for Cubans to use remittances, they must pay a 10% fee to the Cuban government to convert foreign currency to their local currency, the Cuban convertible peso (CUC). This means the Cuban government extracts $300 million each year from families needing financial assistance from their relatives living overseas.[1] To make matters worse, on September 6, 2019, the United States cut off dollar-denominated remittances to Cuba, removing a vital economic lifeline for Cuban families.[10] With this ban, Cubans no longer have access to American-made financial services such as Venmo and PayPal.

Starting in January 2021, the Communist Party of Cuba began a process known as "monetary purification" to terminate the CUC in place of a new system known as the MLC, or "freely convertible currency." On the 1st of the year, the Cuban government began phasing out the CUC, giving Cubans six months to exchange their CUCs for pesos at an official rate. Because the official exchange rate was set at a 15% discount to the free market rate, conversion represented a massive tax on Cuban savings.

As Cuban pesos flooded the market during this exchange, CUCs experienced massive devaluation, losing 75% of their purchasing power. In 2020, a pound of rice cost six pesos, but by the summer of 2021, the same rice cost more than 50 pesos.[1]

In place of the CUC, the Cuban government encouraged the use of the MLC system. Under this system, Cubans receive a reusable money card that can be topped up from a bank or mobile app. Government-run MLC stores are the only places where high-quality food, cleaning supplies, appliances, and medicine can be bought, in effect forcing Cubans to adopt the new system. The catch is that Cubans cannot use their pesos to purchase MLC credit—they can only top up their accounts with foreign currency. This means they need family contacts abroad to send them funds or must purchase foreign currency on the black market at a steeper price. This process allows the Cuban government to freely print new pesos anytime the Cuban people exchange their hard currency, using money printing to tax its people. Just as Africans are stuck under the economic regime of the CFA franc, Cubans are trapped in a monetary system that continually keeps them economically repressed.

Just as Africans such as Fodé Diop began using Bitcoin to escape the franc, so too have Cubans turned to Bitcoin to escape a devaluing peso and repressive MLC system. In his book *Check Your Financial Privilege*, Alex Gladstein researched Cuba to understand the emergence of Bitcoin. He spoke with a Cuban healthcare worker named Lucia, who described Bitcoin as her best option for saving money for the future. To Lucia, "Bitcoin allows you to control your money, your spending, and by extension, your life. As a woman, my future is finally in my own hands."[1] In a country where machismo and misogyny are felt everywhere, Lucia says that Bitcoin is essential for women to gain control over their finances.

For these reasons, according to Cruz, a Cuban state TV personality and YouTuber who creates videos for Cubans about technology and payment systems, "The number of Cubans using Bitcoin is exploding."[1] He estimates that more than 300,000 Cubans, or roughly 2.5% of the Cuban population, have used Bitcoin. In his opinion, Cubans are turning to Bitcoin because they trust it for their savings more than the Cuban peso. This growth has resulted in a burgeoning Bitcoin economy within Cuba. Cruz founded BitRemesas, a company allowing families to send bitcoin between the US and Cuba, circumventing the ban on dollar remittance payments. Using a company called Bitrefill, Cubans can pay for their phone bill and make purchases on their phone using bitcoin. Other services empower taxi drivers and apartment owners to receive foreign payments facilitated by Bitcoin. Collectively, Cubans recognize the value of bitcoin because it offers a tremendous improvement over the other financial services available to them.[1]

Like Africans living within the CFA, with Bitcoin, Cubans can now reliably save for the future. With just an internet connection and a mobile device, Cubans finally have the power to escape an oppressive monetary regime. While it is difficult for Westerners to see the value of Bitcoin because they have the luxury of living in a relatively equitable financial system, when presented with Bitcoin, Cubans immediately understand its importance to the world. Jorge, a Havana resident and avid Bitcoiner, describes its value in the eyes of Cubans:

> This technology goes around blockades and government restrictions, it allows you to move value without trusting anyone, it connects you to the world, and it allows you to empower yourself and do things that are otherwise impossible. It has created hope for those who want change.[1]

Remittances

Just as the Cuban people rely on remittance payments for much of their income, so too do 800 million people worldwide.[11] In 2023, roughly $860 billion of remittance payments were sent globally,[12] with 75% of these funds spent on essential items such as food, school supplies, and medical care. Globally, 16 countries derive at least 20% of their economic output from remittances alone.[13] However, despite the size of the remittance market and the growth of the internet, remittance payments still face high fees (6% on average) and payment delays of days to weeks.[14] This means that more than $50 billion—a figure twice the size of El Salvador's economy—is spent every year on payment fees, money that would otherwise be in the hands of impoverished families. Thankfully, with the growth and development of Bitcoin, people around the world can instantly receive money from their loved ones at a small fraction of the cost.

Sudan exemplifies a nation in desperate need of improved remittances. Since a political coup in 1989, Omar al-Bashir has ruled the country with an authoritarian grip. In the early 2000s, mass genocide occurred against the Sudanese people under his command, where he ordered the murder of hundreds of thousands and displaced millions more. He instituted a monetary police force that froze bank accounts, confiscated Sudanese assets, and seized the savings of many Sudanese citizens. Due to his financial mismanagement, the country faced 340% inflation in 2021. As a result, the Sudanese are completely shut off from the Western monetary system, lacking access to payment apps and other financial solutions.

Yet, with the rise of Bitcoin, Sudanese citizens with a phone and access to the internet can store their wealth in an asset that can't be confiscated by al-Bashir's monetary police and can receive remittance payments from family abroad. According to a Sudanese doctor named Mo, Bitcoin is a "lifeline" to many Sudanese still trapped in the country. He now lives in Europe and uses Bitcoin to send money to his friends and family back in Sudan, enabling him to circumvent fees and seizures from the government.[1]

In Ethiopia, people are also turning to Bitcoin as a lifeline. Today, the country has a population of 130 million, 55% of whom have no access to a bank account.[15] In some places of the country, salt is still used as a currency because they lack access to a modern monetary system. Ethiopians face 20% annual inflation and do not trust that their currency, the birr, will hold value over time, leading some to use cattle and sheep to store value. To receive remittance payments through classic providers such as Western Union, Ethiopians must pay 13% fees just to receive their money.

Because of these problems, Bitcoin is now used throughout Ethiopia to save for the future and receive remittance payments. Kal Kassa, an Ethiopian businessman, regularly uses Bitcoin, believing its adoption will spread quickly throughout the country, which is rapidly gaining access to the internet.[1]

While remittance payments are a foreign concept to many living in Western countries, they are the lifeline for many impoverished families who lack access to stable currencies, modern financial services, and consistent employment. Their broad and continued use, despite the high fees and delays, is a testament to their importance. Bitcoin proves to be a substantial improvement over the status quo, as fees to send bitcoin are often as low as 0.1%, and senders have certainty that their transactions will be made within minutes, not hours or days. As such, remittance payments sent with bitcoin exemplify how Bitcoin is a step-function improvement over our current financial system. While inflation, a lack of transparency and predictability, and unnecessary complexity are the norm in today's financial world, Bitcoin proves that these are not inherent properties of money but are symptoms of a broken and antiquated system.

While it may be difficult for Westerners to appreciate the importance of Bitcoin to the future health of our society, this case does not need to be made to millions worldwide. Roya Mahboob understands how traditional financial systems oppress women and how Bitcoin offers freedom for women globally. Those trapped in the CFA, including Chad's President Déby and entrepreneur Fodé, recognize that monetary systems are still used to extract wealth from the many into the hands of the few and see Bitcoin as a way to escape monetary colonialism. People like Lucia, Cruz, and Jorge in Cuba appreciate how a broken medium of exchange prevents people from saving for the future and how Bitcoin offers a compelling solution. Dr. Mo from Sudan and Kal Kassa in Ethiopia understand the brokenness of our current payment system and how Bitcoin offers a payment rail that provides a significant improvement over what currently exists. Millions of such individuals are living proof that if we can fix our money, we can take a first step toward fixing the world.

BITCOIN NUANCES

Throughout this book, we have shown how money evolves according to a set of principles. In this sense, money's evolution appears to have been predictable. Was it a coincidence that gold emerged organically in multiple societies, independently, throughout humanity's development? We hope that after reading this book, readers understand that money's evolution wasn't random. Indeed, if a simulation of societal development over millennia was run 10,000 times, it is likely that gold would emerge as the chosen money in a vast majority of cases.

Likewise, consider a similar simulation, this time featuring a modern fiat money system. It is likely that, in most cases, the given form of fiat money would become obsolete within a century. This is because while technology may change throughout history, human desires and behavior remain constant. In scenarios where governments have the ability to debase their currency for a short term gain, history shows they are likely to do so repeatedly. As a result, predicting the future path of any given fiat money system is a straightforward exercise. After all, every recorded instance of hyperinflation, where a currency's value quickly drops to zero, has occurred under a fiat standard. Moreover, governments with excessive debt burdens predictably default on such obligations; since 1800, 51 out of 52 countries with a total debt load 30% greater than the size of their economy have defaulted,* either outright or via printing money.[1]

While the trajectories of past monies appear predictable in hindsight, the future remains uncertain. The money that will emerge in the 21st century, whether that be Bitcoin or otherwise, is not preordained. Many factors at play have real consequences on the adoption of such a technology. Therefore, acknowledging Bitcoin's potential limitations is essential in this context.

As previously outlined, Bitcoin's growth closely resembles the trajectories of the internet and personal computers. In all three cases, the swift proliferation of a new type of technology brings with it a wave of opportunistic behaviors. Inevitably, some individuals try to reap quick profits by exploiting the naivety of

---

* A default is the failure to make payments on a debt.

those unfamiliar with the technology. The rapid adoption of the internet in the late 1990s was paired with a stock market bubble, where the tech-heavy NASDAQ index rose by 582% between January 1995 and March 2000.[2] The immense returns seen in the stock market created a fervor of financial speculation on internet-related companies. Alongside such fervor came a litany of fraud and scams, taking advantage of a public that had not yet been informed on the internet.

Bitcoin's rise has been nothing short of extraordinary, surpassing even the most successful stories from the dot-com boom. It is no secret that surrounding the rise of Bitcoin, there have been many adjacent cases of financial speculation gone wrong. This has manifested in social media scams, pump-and-dump schemes, celebrity endorsements of questionable assets, data breaches, hacks, online platforms promising unrealistically high returns on cryptocurrencies, and fraudulent exchanges. Collectively, these schemes have led to consumer losses exceeding $10 billion, highlighting the need for caution and awareness in this evolving financial landscape.

The year 2022 witnessed a significant 64% decline in Bitcoin's price, with numerous instances of fraud in the cryptocurrency sector being unearthed. None were as colossal or rapid as the downfall of FTX, a major crypto exchange. Founded only three years earlier by 27-year-old Sam Bankman-Fried, FTX had quickly risen to become the world's fourth-largest crypto exchange, boasting a valuation exceeding $30 billion.[3] The platform attracted millions of users who entrusted it with their cryptocurrency deposits, including bitcoin.

Eventually, it was uncovered that Bankman-Fried had been siphoning off customer funds for extravagant expenses, including Caribbean real estate and political contributions. The crisis erupted in November 2022, spurred by fears of FTX's insolvency, which led to a massive withdrawal of deposits. This run on the exchange revealed an $8 billion shortfall in funds owed to customers. A year later, Sam Bankman-Fried was convicted on seven criminal charges and now sits behind bars.[4]

The harm caused by the collapses of FTX and other fraudulent businesses damages the trust that is placed in bitcoin and other cryptocurrencies. Although unrelated to the fundamental operations of the Bitcoin network, this loss of trust represents a threat to Bitcoin's future adoption if high-profile cases of fraud continue.

After the dot-com mania in the late 1990s, the stock market decline between 2000 and 2002 similarly unearthed cases of fraud and bankruptcies. WorldCom, once known for the largest bankruptcy in US history, stands as an example of a company that took advantage of financial fervor despite having little value to offer. Despite these calamities and the decline of the stock market, the internet continued to operate as normal in the early 2000s, its adoption spreading exponentially. Likewise, the Bitcoin network continues to operate as normal in the wake of such crimes as FTX, its adoption spreading each year.

It's crucial to distinguish that the scams, frauds, and dubious business practices prevalent in the wider cryptocurrency industry do not reflect on the Bitcoin network, which remains uncompromised and untainted by malicious activities. Similar to the internet in the year 2000, the Bitcoin network continues to adhere to its predefined code, regularly processing transactions without interruption. Just as the internet grew to be a network trusted by billions, the Bitcoin network is following a similar trajectory of growth and acceptance into the mainstream financial services industry. Today, while Bitcoin remains in the early stages of its adoption, it's crucial to be educated about what Bitcoin can promise, as well as its nuances and best practices.

Careful Consideration of Existing Skepticism

Given its novelty and rapid growth, Bitcoin warrants thorough scrutiny and in-depth examination. However, some of the most widely voiced concerns raised about Bitcoin prove unfounded upon closer inspection. This kind of skepticism is common with new technologies. For instance, during the internet's early days, the "Y2K Bug" sparked widespread fear, suggesting that the arrival of the year 2000 would lead to significant computer failures—a concern that was ultimately more speculative than factual. The subsequent sections will address five such considerations about Bitcoin. Additional information and resources for the inquisitive reader are also provided at TheRevolutionofMoney.com.

Consideration #1: Bitcoin wastes energy

The security of the Bitcoin network is ultimately derived from real-world consumption of energy. Commodity monies of the past were all similar in this respect. The process of mining gold, producing new cowrie shells, or creating more wampum was an energy-intensive process. This burden is what keeps commodities scarce; if mining gold didn't require the output of much energy, the venture of gold mining would be extremely profitable for a time, leading to a rapid expansion of the gold mining industry and thus the rapid expansion of gold's supply.

Bitcoin's architecture mirrors this principle of commodity money by explicitly connecting money with energy through a process called bitcoin "mining." Bitcoin miners are responsible for securing the Bitcoin network and creating new blocks of transactions. Each transaction block is submitted by a single miner, who is compensated with bitcoin.* To earn the right to submit the next block of transactions and therefore receive bitcoin as compensation, bitcoin miners compete to be the first to correctly cryptographically hash (i.e., encode) the next block of transactions (note that blocks must also adhere to the network's predefined rules in order to be accepted by the network). Correctly encoding each new block requires spending energy as computational power. The security of the Bitcoin network is founded on such energy expenditure. The real-world cost associated with

---

* The bitcoin rewards received by miners come from transaction fees and Bitcoin's pre-defined monetary schedule, which slowly releases new bitcoin into the network until reaching its 21 million cap in the year 2140.

creating each new block also serves as a real-world deterrent for any attacks on the network. Due to the rewards that come with creating a block, bitcoin mining is a highly competitive endeavor, rendering it exceedingly unlikely for a malicious actor to compromise the network. There are hundreds of public and private bitcoin mining companies focused entirely on building out computational capacity to mine bitcoin. The sheer size and distributed nature of the bitcoin mining industry serve as significant deterrents to any attempts at network corruption.

Due to the energy-intensive nature of bitcoin mining, a variety of concerns exist about the necessity of such energy use, its sources, and its impacts. These concerns generally fall into three categories:

1) Bitcoin's energy use is wasteful.
2) Bitcoin is harmful to the environment.
3) Bitcoin's energy use comes at the expense of other economic actors.

Upon further examination, it becomes clear that Bitcoin's energy use is foundational to its functioning as money, that such energy use incentivizes the build-out of more sustainable sources of electricity, and that the nature of Bitcoin's energy consumption benefits the stability and robustness of electrical grids. The following section will briefly cover these points.

First, Bitcoin's use of energy is what ultimately gives the network security and, therefore, value. If not for bitcoin mining, there would be no monetary system exhibiting the same qualities needed in a 21st-century medium of exchange. As such, the societal benefit that is derived from Bitcoin far outweighs its energy cost— which in 2022 was estimated to be 0.04% of global energy consumption.[5] To put this in perspective, Bitcoin uses one-fourth and one-twentieth the amount of energy required to power YouTube and air conditioning, respectively.[6,7]

Compared to traditional forms of monetary extraction such as gold mining, bitcoin mining is significantly less carbon-intensive, generating less than a third of the carbon emissions produced by the gold mining industry today. When comparing Bitcoin with the current monetary system, while it is hard to directly compare environmental impact, Bitcoin has far fewer societal and economic costs than the US dollar. These include the cost of the US military to maintain the status of its fiat money as a reserve currency, the detrimental impacts of inflation, and the numerous economic inefficiencies that come from a financial system built around an unpredictable and opaque form of money.

Despite its energy consumption, the security provided by bitcoin mining is a worthwhile trade-off for the decentralized and trust-minimized system it upholds, distinguishing it from the traditional fiat system with its centralized control and associated economic costs.

Second, bitcoin mining improves the economics of renewable energy production by enabling power production in remote locations and providing stability to otherwise volatile power demand. Bitcoin mining is an operation that can be done anywhere on the planet. Unlike other industries, a bitcoin mining facility does not need to be located directly on a power grid or within a populated area. Drew Armstrong and AJ Scalia from the public bitcoin miner Cathedra elaborate on this point:

> Bitcoin mining directly incentivizes new and more efficient forms of energy generation by offering a "bounty" to anyone, anywhere, at any time, who finds a cheaper way to produce energy at scale. This direct financial incentive for more efficient generation and the newfound viability of previously uneconomical sources of energy will cause a

general decline in the price of energy worldwide.[8]

The distinct incentive structure within bitcoin mining, which prioritizes finding the most cost-effective energy sources globally, makes low-emission sources such as nuclear, wind, solar, hydroelectric, and methane gas flaring particularly attractive for this industry. A 2022 report by KPMG underscores the potential role of Bitcoin in fostering a sustainable future:

> The sun is only out for a portion of the day and wind output is variable, often peaking during the evening. Additionally, renewable energy facilities are incentivized to produce at their maximum capacity to deliver electricity in a manner consistent with their contractual agreements. This can leave utilities with an excess supply of electricity, which if coupled with a supply and demand mismatch, can lead to low, and even negative, electricity prices.
>
> Bitcoin miners can setup anywhere, including co-locating around these renewable energy sources, offering a flexible load that can work in harmony with supply and demand patterns.

This ability for bitcoin miners to dynamically flex their power consumption during periods of excess supply and/or low market demand can provide additional incentive to the buildout of additional renewable energy capacity. These non-core load centers improve the economics of renewable energy projects by allowing their developers to facilitate further expansion of their operations. Former CEO of ERCOT, which operates the bulk energy system in the state of Texas, Brad Jones, stated in a recent public appearance that "Bitcoin allows those renewables to earn money during those times rather than having to shut off their service, or even having to pay customers to use their power" and "Bitcoin mining helps to sustain those markets for renewables and drives more renewables."

It's worth noting that Texas produces far more renewable energy than any other state in the country, having produced over 136,000 gigawatt hours of wind and solar energy in 2022. As a result, it's not surprising that Texas has become a popular destination for Bitcoin miners and represents approximately 59% of the total Bitcoin hash rate volume in the United States.[9]

In essence, bitcoin miners improve the economics of renewable power plants by consuming excess power that would otherwise be wasted during periods of low demand. In turn, this enables renewable energy companies to increase their production capabilities, allowing them to capitalize on sunny or windy periods.

A 2022 paper co-authored by Brad Jones demonstrates that aside from renewable energy sources, bitcoin mining could account for 3.0% of the annual emissions reduction target in America's oil and gas sector by reducing flare gas emissions, with the following rationale:

> Innovative bitcoin miners have strategically positioned themselves to harness unconventional energy sources, highlighting the adaptability inherent in the mining process. Given the modest infrastructure demands of bitcoin mining, predominantly relying on electricity and specialized ASIC hardware, miners possess the latitude to explore energy sources beyond traditional grids and internet infrastructure. This strategic positioning becomes feasible in the

presence of accessible and low-cost energy sources, and Starlink internet connections. Among these unconventional sources, flared methane, a byproduct of oil extraction processes and potent greenhouse gas, emerges as an important use case because of the high international priority given to mitigating methane emissions. In situations where pipelines are absent or transportation proves uneconomical, surplus natural gas is frequently vented or flared at well-pads, contributing to substantial CO2e emissions. In 2021 alone, 140 billion cubic meters of gas were flared or vented, contributing >300-m tonnes of CO2e to the atmosphere. A pioneering approach within the Bitcoin mining community involves the utilization of electricity generated from waste methane. Miners are increasingly installing generators at oil fields, turning a one time waste asset into a valuable resource.[7]

Because burning methane to produce power releases fewer greenhouse gasses than simply flaring it or releasing it directly into the atmosphere, bitcoin mining offers a viable solution to reducing methane emissions produced by trash dumps and oil extraction.

It is now estimated that 59.5% of the electricity consumed by the bitcoin mining industry comes from renewable sources, making it one of the greenest industries globally.[10] This figure is likely to increase as the lowest-cost sources of new power will continue to come from renewable sources that generate variable electricity loads.

Lastly, the flexible nature of bitcoin mining benefits the stability and robustness of electrical grids. Electrical grids today source an increasing amount of power from renewable sources, such as wind and solar, which introduce challenges tied to their unpredictability. After all, the sun doesn't always shine, and the wind doesn't always blow. This intermittent power production can pose risks to the stability of electrical grids, particularly during times when the demand for electricity is high while the supply of electricity produced from renewable sources is limited. Bitcoin miners can alleviate these risks, according to Brad Jones et al., in that they emerge "as a uniquely adaptable category […] demonstrating remarkable flexibility and the ability to curtail their energy consumption in a controlled manner with minimal latency over extended periods."[7]

When power prices spike during an adverse event such as a winter storm in Texas, bitcoin miners are unique in their ability to rapidly curtail energy usage, allowing the electrical grid to stabilize.[11] For example, bitcoin miners located in Texas have frequently turned off their machines during winter storms and other adverse events, returning enough power to heat 1.5 million homes.[11]

It would be one thing if bitcoin mining used significant amounts of energy from carbon-heavy sources, raising the power prices for average citizens, all for a seemingly futile objective. Instead, the reality is that bitcoin mining fulfills a tangible and essential role by ensuring the security and dependability of digital currency while simultaneously pioneering innovative approaches that enhance the efficiency and quality of our electrical grids and energy sources.

Consideration #2: Bitcoin is too volatile

The price of bitcoin has been known to swing rapidly to the upside and downside. Despite bitcoin's extraordinary appreciation throughout its short history, its price has fallen by 70% or more on four separate occasions. Naturally, this price volatility has prompted numerous critiques of bitcoin's potential role as money: If bitcoin's price changes so rapidly, how can anyone trust it to be a reliable store of value?

Indeed, there is plenty of truth to this critique. An ideal money should have a relatively stable value to garner trust from its users. For bitcoin to succeed as money, it must eventually achieve a state where its value does not swing to the extent it currently does.

It must be understood, however, that for a money to emerge organically from nothing, it will necessarily have extreme volatility during the early periods of its adoption. In other words, any scenario where bitcoin successfully becomes global money is one mired in price volatility, at least for the early periods of its adoption cycle.

Bitcoin's volatility today is a function of three factors:

1) Bitcoin is early in its adoption phase. As the number of Bitcoin users grows exponentially, its price will experience volatility as a result of this growth.

2) Bitcoin's probability of becoming global money is uncertain. Its price reflects this uncertainty, which can swing rapidly due to macroeconomic, political, and geopolitical events.

3) Bitcoin's price is affected by broader economic conditions. Bitcoin's attractiveness as an investment can vary depending on macroeconomic conditions, such as the rate of

inflation and the level of fiscal restraint seen in our politicians.

The logic behind the first two points suggests that as Bitcoin gains more widespread adoption and its future role becomes clear, its volatility will decrease. A broad and more established user base will contribute to stabilizing its value through several mechanisms. First, as the value of bitcoin increases, the transactions it handles will represent a smaller fraction of its total value, meaning individual transactions will have less impact on its price. Second, the inclusion of bitcoin in millions of professionally managed investment portfolios will help moderate large price swings as the market for buying and selling bitcoin becomes more efficient.

Most importantly, Bitcoin's emergence as a global currency implies that it will increasingly be viewed not as a high-risk investment or speculative asset, but rather as a means for long-term saving, aligning its usage more closely with that of traditional currencies. As described in the third point above, Bitcoin is currently treated by some investors as a way to make bets on specific macroeconomic outcomes, such as a rapid rise in inflation. As Bitcoin continues to be treated more as a form of money instead of as an investment tool for making macroeconomic bets, its price volatility will stabilize.

Years will pass before bitcoin achieves a level of stability comparable to "traditional" forms of money. In this transitional period, individuals and investors should be aware of the potential for significant fluctuations in bitcoin's value. As with any investment, especially in emerging technologies or assets, there's a degree of risk that should be carefully considered.

Consideration #3: Bitcoin will be banned by governments

Despite calls by a select number of domestic and foreign politicians to ban Bitcoin through the political apparatus, such an outcome is unlikely. Numerous countries have already attempted to ban Bitcoin, including Algeria, Bangladesh, Bolivia, Ecuador, Egypt, India, Iran, Kyrgyzstan, Morocco, Nepal, Nigeria, Saudi Arabia, Thailand, and Turkey.[12] However, these bans had little effect and, in most cases, were reversed as governments realized that Bitcoin adoption would not be affected by government regulation.

One such instance is the case of Nigeria, whose central bank—the Central Bank of Nigeria (CBN)—prohibited institutions from facilitating bitcoin transactions in 2017. Despite this directive, the dollar value of bitcoin transacted by Nigerians continued to rise. Then, in February 2021, the CBN ordered banks to "identify persons and/or entities" who were conducting transactions in bitcoin or running crypto exchanges and "ensure that such accounts are closed immediately."[13] These actions by the central bank achieved little in dampening Bitcoin adoption; the country's persistently high inflation rates in excess of 15% were enough to incentivize the adoption of Bitcoin, despite the discouragement from the government. In 2023, the CBN capitulated by lifting bans on facilitating bitcoin transactions.[14] As of the latest estimations, some 16% of Nigerian citizens have reported owning bitcoin.[15]

The only country where a Bitcoin ban would have a material impact on global adoption is the United States, which is incidentally positioned to benefit enormously from this new form of money. Avik Roy, an entrepreneur and senior adviser at the Bipartisan Policy Center, expands on this idea in his essay *Bitcoin and the U.S. Fiscal Reckoning*:

> A bitcoin crackdown would also be a massive strategic mistake, given that Americans are positioned to benefit enormously from bitcoin-related ventures and decentralized

finance more generally. Around 50 million Americans own bitcoin today, and it's likely that Americans and U.S. institutions own a plurality, if not the majority, of the bitcoin in circulation—a sum worth hundreds of billions of dollars. This is one area where China simply cannot compete with the United States, since Bitcoin's open financial architecture is fundamentally incompatible with Beijing's centralized, authoritarian model.

In the absence of major entitlement reform, well-intentioned efforts to make Treasury bonds great again are likely doomed. Instead of restricting bitcoin in a desperate attempt to forestall the inevitable, federal policymakers would do well to embrace the role of bitcoin as a geopolitically neutral reserve asset; work to ensure that the United States continues to lead the world in accumulating bitcoin-based wealth, jobs, and innovations; and ensure that Americans can continue to use bitcoin to protect themselves against government-driven inflation.[16]

Nations are increasingly recognizing the permanence of Bitcoin, realizing that embracing its adoption is a more strategic approach than resisting it. This shift is reflected in the numerous regulatory adjustments that are clarifying the rules for Bitcoin usage around the world. This includes Europe, with the MiCA regulatory framework passed in 2023; the UK, with comprehensive regulation expected in 2024 under the Financial Conduct Authority (FCA); and Asia, with pro-Bitcoin regulation passed in Singapore, Hong Kong, Taiwan, and other jurisdictions. Furthermore, in the United States, several presidential candidates and members of Congress have publicly expressed support for Bitcoin. Ultimately, a country cannot "ban" Bitcoin; they can only ban themselves from taking part in a rapidly growing and transformative technology.

Consideration #4: Bitcoin is a haven for illicit activity

Bitcoin, a universally accessible and open form of money, is equally usable by both ethical and unethical actors, much like cash. Both cash and Bitcoin are impartial tools for exchanging and preserving value, offering significant societal benefits, yet they can be misused due to their resistance to censorship. However, it's important to note that evidence of Bitcoin as a sanctuary for illicit activities is not only limited but has been decreasing over time. Global asset manager Fidelity has highlighted this decline:

> It is important not to consider Bitcoin's use in illicit activity in a vacuum. According to data from blockchain analytics firm Elliptic, bitcoin's use in illicit activities (e.g., dark markets, ransomware, fraudulent activity) has been on a downward trajectory and transactions connected to illicit activity made up less than 1% of total bitcoin transactions in recent years. Bitcoin's transparent nature allows us to establish a concrete estimate of bitcoin's use for illicit activity in a way that we cannot for fiat currencies making it easier to point fingers at bitcoin for facilitating criminal activity, while ignoring the role that cash as well as the financial system play in criminal activity. For example, for every dollar spent in bitcoin on the darknet, at least $800 was laundered via cash, according to The United Nations Drugs and Crime Office and Chainalysis.
>
> "Although virtual currencies are used for illicit transactions, the volume is small compared to the volume of illicit activity through traditional financial services." —

Jennifer Fowler, US Department of the Treasury

The revelation that law enforcement can detect and punish criminal activity with the help of blockchain forensics may also present a barrier to the use of bitcoin by bad actors. Bitcoin is pseudonymous, not anonymous, and blockchain analytics firms have developed sophisticated techniques to trace criminal activity via Bitcoin to real world identities. Additionally, the focus and scrutiny on Bitcoin from regulators and regulated institutions who have the duty to monitor for illicit transactions is only growing as Bitcoin becomes more financialized.[17]

Thus, Bitcoin demonstrates superiority over traditional financial institutions concerning illicit finance. Not only is illicit activity significantly more prevalent in traditional mediums like cash, but the inherent design of our current financial system also facilitates such activities. Since 2000, six leading Wall Street banks have accumulated more than $200 billion in penalties for misconduct, including facilitating money laundering, customer overcharges, creation of unauthorized accounts, and unjustified credit card fee increases.[18] Despite these frequent violations, it's uncommon for the individuals involved to face legal repercussions. The lack of transparency in traditional banking often conceals such activities from regulatory and public oversight. Therefore, when examining Bitcoin for its role in such activities, it is vital to contextualize it with the shortcomings of our current financial system in curbing illicit finance.

Some degree of fraud is a certainty under any monetary or financial system. That being the case, it is worth comparing the degree to which such activity exists across various systems. From 2017 to 2022, there was a stark contrast in the scale of money laundering between traditional currencies and Bitcoin: An estimated $20 trillion has been laundered using fiat currencies, compared to $33 billion in Bitcoin.* The essential role of money is not to restrict who can use it or to dictate which transactions are permissible. Instead, the responsibility to define and enforce these standards lies with democratically elected officials and law enforcement agencies.

While it is easy for anti-Bitcoin politicians to accuse Bitcoin of facilitating illicit activity, providing

---

* We recognize that a more accurate comparison is the % of transaction volume that is laundered money. However, this data is not accurately available, and thus we must compare absolute amounts of money laundering between USD and Bitcoin.

hard evidence for such claims within a broader context is a different story. Bitcoin does not promote illicit activity any more than the US dollar and even offers certain advantages over the dollar system in this regard. Nonetheless, illicit activity such as money laundering and terrorist financing should be prevented as much as possible within all monetary systems, including Bitcoin.

Consideration #5: Bitcoin will be replaced by other cryptocurrencies

As a cryptocurrency, Bitcoin is often compared with other public blockchains, such as Ethereum or Solana. Bitcoin shares some similarities with other blockchains, such as a degree of decentralization and (in most cases) an integrated token. However, these comparisons can be misleading, as Bitcoin's primary function as a form of money sets it apart from other cryptocurrencies focused on different blockchain applications. Its foundational principle of incorruptibility is central to Bitcoin's identity, which is crucial for a reliable monetary system but less critical for blockchains prioritizing varied functionalities.

Bitcoin's primacy as a monetary system is due to three factors:

Bitcoin's purpose: In contrast to the vast majority of blockchains, Bitcoin is uniquely built to function solely as money. The design of its consensus protocol and monetary policy, as well as its core principles of decentralization, incorruptibility, and simplicity, are all in service of positioning Bitcoin as an ideal monetary system.

Blockchains such as Ethereum, Solana, and countless others are developed to support a wide range of applications, sharing some, but not all, of Bitcoin's fundamental values of transparency, incorruptibility, and global accessibility. The likelihood of any blockchain beyond Bitcoin to achieve widespread adoption is beyond the scope of this book. However, it's important to note that the broad acceptance of any such blockchain would not challenge or diminish Bitcoin's fundamental purpose as money of the 21ˢᵗ century.

Bitcoin's monetary policy: Satoshi Nakamoto, the pseudonymous creator of Bitcoin, established a predetermined monetary policy embedded in its code, meant to remain unchanged indefinitely.

As noted in this book, Bitcoin has a mathematically metered supply cap of 21 million. As of this writing, there are 19.7 million bitcoin in existence, leaving the remaining 1.3 million to be distributed through the process of bitcoin mining until the year 2140. The rate at which these remaining coins will be mined is known with precision, meaning that Bitcoin is unique over both fiat currencies and other cryptocurrencies in eliminating unexpected inflation.

While Bitcoin's software has been updated to allow for improved transaction efficiency and other functionalities, its monetary policy is unlikely to change in the future. Bitcoin's predictable and scarce monetary schedule is so core to the network's value that all network participants are incentivized to keep this policy unchanged. Changing Bitcoin's monetary policy would not only require the consensus of a majority of network participants, but would also likely diminish the value of bitcoin itself. These game-theoretical incentives ensure that Bitcoin's monetary schedule is further cemented with each passing year.

For various reasons, other cryptocurrencies do not share such predictability and scarcity in their supply; changes in these networks' supply schedules have repeatedly occurred since inception. While such a change would be detrimental to the Bitcoin network, they are not regarded with the same level of seriousness as other cryptocurrencies because these blockchains do not serve first and foremost as money.

Bitcoin's incorruptibility: Bitcoin's degree of decentralization and incorruptibility, largely stemming from its unique origin story, is unlikely to be paralleled or replicated. After participating in Bitcoin development since its launch in 2009, Satoshi Nakamoto deliberately withdrew from the public sphere in April 2011. This withdrawal was a strategic move that reinforced Bitcoin's decentralized nature. By removing any semblance of central authority or influence associated with a known creator, Nakamoto ensured that Bitcoin would operate without the risk of manipulation or influence from its creator. This scenario is quite common in other cryptocurrencies.

The absence of a central figure has elevated Bitcoin to a distinct position in the realm of digital currencies. Bitcoin is a leaderless entity governed by consensus and the immutable laws set forth in its original code. This level of decentralization and the absence of a controlling authority provide Bitcoin with a degree of incorruptibility and resilience that is rare, if not impossible, to replicate in other cryptocurrencies.

In this regard, comparing Bitcoin with the second-largest cryptocurrency, Ethereum, is useful. Ethereum launched in 2014, pioneering the use of "smart contracts" on a blockchain. Ethereum attempts to provide a broad range of decentralized services unrelated to the core functions of money. In contrast to Bitcoin, Ethereum's founding team is publicly known, with several members actively involved in its ongoing development. Upon Ethereum's launch, the founding team allocated 9.9% of the total token supply to themselves, primarily to fund the development of numerous network "upgrades." This centralization of supply is significant, especially in light of Ethereum's consensus mechanism.

Unlike Bitcoin's mining-based system (known as proof-of-work), Ethereum's consensus model is predicated on the amount of Ethereum one possesses (proof-of-stake), meaning those with larger holdings have more influence over the network. While this framework aligns with Ethereum's emphasis on non-monetary functionalities, it undermines its suitability as a currency, primarily due to a heightened risk of corruption.

Beyond Ethereum, many thousands of other cryptocurrencies created after Bitcoin bear the imprint of their founders, often publicly known and actively involved in their governance. This ongoing involvement of founders introduces a potential for influence and change, which, while it may benefit innovation and adaptation, also opens the door to corruptibility and centralization. Such dynamics starkly differentiate these cryptocurrencies from Bitcoin, which stands alone in its incorruptible nature, largely due to Nakamoto's strategic retreat from the public domain.

What's Next?

This book sought to provide an introduction to money's past and ongoing evolution. Numerous topics concerning both our current monetary system and Bitcoin were not covered exhaustively. Therefore, curious readers are encouraged to continue learning about the inner workings of such systems. To that end, various resources are provided at: TheRevolutionofMoney.com.

Finally, readers contemplating the inclusion of bitcoin in their savings are encouraged to take the time to learn about both the benefits and risks of bitcoin, carefully considering what role it may play in a financial portfolio. Bitcoin is designed not for speculative gains or fulfilling short-term desires but rather as a tool for long-term wealth accumulation and, therefore, should be treated as such. Further, readers should note that there are a multitude of ways of acquiring bitcoin, each presenting different levels of security and control over personal assets. The most suitable approach depends on an individual's priorities, along with their technical and financial expertise.

CITATIONS

Introduction

1. Selman, D., & Leighton, P. (2018). Ramen Politics: Informal Money and Logics of Resistance in the Contemporary American Prison. Retrieved from https://www.researchgate.net/publication/325084427_Ramen_Politics_Informal_Money_and_Logics_of_Resistance_in_the_Contemporary_American_Prison.
2. Davies, R. (2019). Extreme Economies: What Life at the World's Margins Can Teach Us About Our Own Future.
3. Federal Reserve Economic Data. FRED.
4. US Census Bureau

Chapter 1

1. Davies, G. (1994). A History of Money from Ancient Times to the Present Day.
2. (1875–1876). Money Changer and a Customer. Wikimedia Commons. Retrieved from https://commons.wikimedia.org/wiki/File:Money_Changer_and_a_Customer_(note_the_usage_of_Cowrie_Shells_as_small_change)_-_1875-1876.jpg.
3. Szabo, N. (2002). Shelling Out: The Origins of Money. Nakamoto Institute. Retrieved from https://nakamotoinstitute.org/shelling-out/.
4. Dunbar, R. 1992. Neocortex size as a constraint on group size in primates. Retrieved from https://www.sciencedirect.com/science/article/abs/pii/004724849290081J.

5. Szabo, N. (2017). Money, blockchains, and social scalability. Retrieved from https://unenumerated.blogspot.com/2017/02/money-blockchains-and-social-scalability.html.

6. Harari, Y. N. (2014). Sapiens: A Brief History of Humankind. Harper.

7. Ferguson, N. (2008). The Ascent of Money: A Financial History of the World. Penguin Books.

8. Vogelvluchtgezicht op de Beurs van Hendrik de Keyser te Amsterdam Byrsa Amsterodamensis. Wikimedia Commons. Retrieved from https://commons.wikimedia.org/wiki/File:Vogelvluchtgezi cht_op_de_Beurs_van_Hendrik_de_Keyser_te_Amsterda m_Byrsa_Amsterodamensis_(titel_op_object),_RP-P-1880-A-3841.jpg.

9. Wooldridge, A., & Micklethwait, J. (2003). The Company: A Short History of a Revolutionary Idea.

10. Dalio, R. (2020). Principles for Dealing with the Changing World Order: Why Nations Succeed and Fail. Simon & Schuster.

Chapter 2

1. Library of Congress. Discovery of Gold. California First Person Narratives. Retrieved from https://www.loc.gov/collections/california-first-person-narratives/articles-and-essays/early-california-history/discovery-of-gold/.

2. History.com Editors. (2022, August 10). California Gold Rush. HISTORY. A&E Television Networks. Retrieved from https://www.history.com/topics/19th-century/gold-rush-of-1849.

3. California Gold Rush handbill. Wikimedia Commons. Retrieved from https://commons.wikimedia.org/wiki/File:California_Gold_Rush_handbill.jpg.

4. PBS. California Gold Rush. American Experience. Retrieved from https://www.pbs.org/wgbh/americanexperience/features/goldrush-california/.

5. Davies, G. (1994). A History of Money.

6. Harari, Y. N. (2014). Sapiens: A Brief History of Humankind. Harper.

7. Ammous, S. (2018). The Bitcoin Standard: The Decentralized Alternative to Central Banking. Wiley.

8. Alden, L. (2022). Broken Money. Saif House.

9. Szabo, N. (2002). Shelling Out: The Origins of Money. Nakamoto Institute. Retrieved from https://nakamotoinstitute.org/shelling-out/.

10. Handbook to the ethnographical collections (1910). Wikimedia Commons. Retrieved from https://commons.wikimedia.org/wiki/File:Handbook_to_the_ethnographical_collections_(1910)_(14803144273).jpg.

11. Dawkins, R. (1976). The Selfish Gene. Oxford University Press.

12. Cooper, R. N., Dornbusch, R., & Hall, R. E. (1982). Exchange Rates and Fiscal Policy in a Popular Model of International Trade.

13. Yeager, L. B. (1981, May). The Classical Gold Standard: Some Lessons for Today. Federal Reserve Bank of St. Louis Review, 63(5), 3-13. Retrieved from

https://files.stlouisfed.org/files/htdocs/publications/review/81/05/Classical_May1981.pdf.

Chapter 3

1. The Franklin Institute. Origins of the Telegraph. Retrieved from https://fi.edu/en/blog/origins-telegraph.

2. Library of Congress. Invention of the Telegraph. Samuel Morse Papers. Retrieved from https://www.loc.gov/collections/samuel-morse-papers/articles-and-essays/invention-of-the-telegraph/.

3. Encyclopaedia Britannica. Telegraph. In Encyclopaedia Britannica. Retrieved from https://www.britannica.com/technology/telegraph.

4. Alden, L. (2022). Broken Money. Saif House.

5. Malekan, O. (2022). Re-Architecting Trust.

6. Unknown. US $10,000 1882 Gold Certificate [Image]. Wikimedia Commons. Retrieved from https://commons.wikimedia.org/wiki/File:US_$10,000_1882_Gold_Certificate.jpg.

7. Neary, L. (2011, April 30). WWI: The Battle That Split Europe And Families. NPR. https://www.npr.org/2011/04/30/135803783/wwi-the-battle-that-split-europe-and-families.

8. Lacey, J. (2015). Gold, Blood, and Power: Finance and War Through the Ages.

9. Domonoske, C. (2017, August 8). 'Financial Times' Issues 103-Year-Old Correction. NPR. https://www.npr.org/sections/thetwo-way/2017/08/08/542238978/-financial-times-issues-103-year-old-correction.

10. Ammous, S. (2021). The Fiat Standard. The Saif House.

11. Chadha, J. S. (2017, August 8). Your country needs funds: The extraordinary story of Britain's early efforts to finance the First World War. Bank Underground. Retrieved from https://bankunderground.co.uk/2017/08/08/your-country-needs-funds-the-extraordinary-story-of-britains-early-efforts-to-finance-the-first-world-war/.

12. Ammous, S. (2018). The Bitcoin Standard: The Decentralized Alternative to Central Banking. Wiley.

13. Hülsmann, J. G. (n.d.). Ludwig von Mises on Money and Inflation. Mises Institute. Retrieved from https://cdn.mises.org/Ludwig%20von%20Mises%20on%20Money%20and%20Inflation_2.pdf.

14. Wikimedia Commons. (1923). German Railways Banknote 5 Billionen Mark 1923 Hyperinflation Notgeld Stuttgart, obverse. Retrieved from https://commons.wikimedia.org/wiki/File:German_Railways_Banknote_5_Billionen_Mark_1923_Hyperinflation_Notgeld_Stuttgart,_obverse.jpg.

15. Cicero, M. T. (n.d.). *Cicero (Marcus Tullius Cicero) 106–43 bc Roman orator and statesman.* Oxford Reference. https://www.oxfordreference.com/display/10.1093/acref/9780191826719.001.0001/q-oro-ed4-00003011.

16. Kaplanis, C. (2003). The Debasement of the "Dollar of the Middle Ages." *The Journal of Economic History, 63*(3), 768–801. http://www.jstor.org/stable/3132307.

17. Sussman, N. (1993). Debasements, Royal Revenues, and Inflation in France During the Hundred Years' War, 1415-1422. *The Journal of Economic History, 53*(1), 44–70. http://www.jstor.org/stable/2123175.

18. Bordo, Michael D. and White, Eugene Nelson, British and French Finance During the Napoleonic Wars

(November 1990). NBER Working Paper No. w3517, Available at SSRN: https://ssrn.com/abstract=471515.

19. Rothbard, M. (2002, January 1) A History of Money and Banking: The Colonial Era to World War II. Mises Institute.

Chapter 4

1. Conceptcarz.com. Ford Model T. Retrieved from https://www.conceptcarz.com/s14456/ford-model-t.aspx.

2. Fox, J. (2023, July 17). San Francisco Isn't Destined to Be the Next Detroit. Bloomberg Opinion. Retrieved from https://www.bloomberg.com/opinion/articles/2023-07-17/san-francisco-isn-t-destined-to-be-the-next-detroit.

3. Unknown. (circa 1920). Michigan & Griswold circa 1920 [Photograph]. Wikimedia Commons. Retrieved from https://commons.wikimedia.org/wiki/File:Michigan_%26_Griswold_circa_1920.jpg.

4. US Census Bureau.

5. (1921, February 23). World's oil output increased in 1920. The New York Times. Retrieved from https://www.nytimes.com/1921/02/23/archives/worlds-oil-output-increased-in-1920-total-production-689000000.html.

6. Paul Kennedy, The Rise and Fall of the Great Powers (1987) p. 200.

7. Ammous, S. (2018). The Bitcoin Standard: The Decentralized Alternative to Central Banking. Wiley.

8. Federal Reserve History. Fed's Formative Years. Retrieved from https://www.federalreservehistory.org/essays/feds-formative-years.

9. U.S. Gold Bureau. Gold Confiscation. Retrieved from https://www.usgoldbureau.com/gold-confiscation.

10. Federal Reserve History. Gold Reserve Act. Retrieved from https://www.federalreservehistory.org/essays/gold-reserve-act.

11. Scottsdale Bullion & Coin. A Dangerous Precedent: Executive Order 6102. Retrieved from https://www.sbcgold.com/blog/a-dangerous-precedent-executive-order-6102/.

12. The National WWII Museum. New Global Power After World War II (1945). Retrieved from https://www.nationalww2museum.org/war/articles/new-global-power-after-world-war-ii-1945.

13. Chadha, J. S. (2017, August 8). Your country needs funds: The extraordinary story of Britain's early efforts to finance the First World War. Bank Underground. Retrieved from https://bankunderground.co.uk/2017/08/08/your-country-needs-funds-the-extraordinary-story-of-britains-early-efforts-to-finance-the-first-world-war/.

14. WW2Data. UK National Income and Expenditure 1938-1945. Retrieved from https://ww2data.com/uk-national-income-and-expenditure-1938-1945/.

15. Gladstein, A. (2022). Check Your Financial Privilege. BTC Media.

16. Alden, L. (2023). Broken Money. The Saif House.

17. Gensler, G. (2023, December 4). *"Exorbitant Privilege: Responsibilities and Challenges": Prepared Remarks before the Council on Foreign Relations.* U.S. Securities and Exchange Commission. Retrieved from https://www.sec.gov/news/speech/gensler-prepared-remarks-council-foreign-relations-12042023.

18. National Archives. The Marshall Plan. Retrieved from https://www.archives.gov/milestone-documents/marshall-plan.

19. Naval History and Heritage Command. Costs of Major U.S. Wars. Retrieved from https://www.history.navy.mil/research/library/online-reading-room/title-list-alphabetically/c/costs-major-us-wars.html#costs.

20. Edwards, C. (1999). The Cost of Government. Cato Institute. Retrieved from https://www.cato.org/sites/cato.org/files/pubs/pdf/pa114.pdf.

21. Truman, H. S. (1949). Annual Budget Message to the Congress for Fiscal Year 1950. The American Presidency Project. Retrieved from https://www.presidency.ucsb.edu/documents/annual-budget-message-the-congress-fiscal-year-1950.

22. Ferguson, N. (2008). The Ascent of Money: A Financial History of the World. Penguin Books.

23. Lynch, D. J. (2021, January 15). The Rise and Fall and Rise (and Fall) of the U.S. Financial Empire. Foreign Policy. Retrieved from https://foreignpolicy.com/2021/01/15/rise-fall-united-states-financial-empire-dollar-global-currency/.

24. Graetz, M. (2016). A "Barbarous Relic": The French, Gold, and the Demise of Bretton Woods. Columbia Law School Faculty Scholarship. Retrieved from https://scholarship.law.columbia.edu/faculty_scholarship/2541/.

Chapter 5

1. Alden, L. Fraying petrodollar system. Lyn Alden. Retrieved from https://www.lynalden.com/fraying-petrodollar-system/.

2. Wong, A. (2016, May 30). The Untold Story Behind Saudi Arabia's 41-Year U.S. Debt Secret. Bloomberg. Retrieved from https://www.bloomberg.com/news/features/2016-05-30/the-untold-story-behind-saudi-arabia-s-41-year-u-s-debt-secret.

3. Reuters. (2023, October 20). Strait of Hormuz: the world's most important oil artery. Reuters. Retrieved from https://www.reuters.com/business/energy/strait-hormuz-worlds-most-important-oil-artery-2023-10-20/.

4. OPEC. Data and graphs. Organization of the Petroleum Exporting Countries. Retrieved from https://www.opec.org/opec_web/en/data_graphs/330.htm.

5. Eichengreen, B. (2015). International Currencies Past, Present and Future: Two Views from Economic History. Cambridge University. Retrieved from https://www.inet.econ.cam.ac.uk/events-files/2015/EichengreenInternationalCurrenciesPastPresentandFutureTwoViewsfromEconomicHistory.pdf.

6. Federal Reserve Economic Data. FRED.

7. Economic Policy Institute. (n.d.). Botched policy responses to globalization. Retrieved from https://www.epi.org/publication/botched-policy-responses-to-globalization/.

8. Richter, W. (2019, October 5). GM, Ford, BMW, VW, Honda Shift More Production to Mexico. Auto Imports

Surge Despite Decline in US Sales. Wolf Street. Retrieved from https://wolfstreet.com/2019/10/05/us-auto-imports-from-mexico-surge-even-as-us-sales-fall-gm-ford-bmw-vw-honda-others-shift-more-production-to-mexico/.

9. Lahart, J. (2011). Number of the Week: Finance's Share of Economy Continues to Grow. The Wall Street Journal. Retrieved from https://www.wsj.com/articles/BL-REB-15342.

10. Yago, G. Junk Bonds. Library of Economics and Liberty (Econlib). Retrieved from https://www.econlib.org/library/Enc/JunkBonds.html.

11. Cleghorn, J. (1989). REYNOLDS TOBACCO TRIMS STAFF. The Washington Post. Retrieved from https://www.washingtonpost.com/archive/business/1989/08/11/reynolds-tobacco-trims-staff/be8b3f73-6e53-4832-a7dc-3168358a0918/.

12. US Census Bureau.

13. Feygin, Y. (2020). The Class Politics of the Dollar System. Phenomenal World. Retrieved from https://www.phenomenalworld.org/analysis/the-class-politics-of-the-dollar-system/.

14. Wiggins, Rosalind Z.; Piontek, Thomas; and Metrick, Andrew. (2019). The Lehman Brothers Bankruptcy A: Overview. Journal of Financial Crises: Vol. 1 : Iss. 1, 39-62. Available at: https://elischolar.library.yale.edu/journal-of-financial-crises/vol1/iss1/2.

15. Pandemic Response Accountability Committee. Paycheck Protection Program (PPP). Retrieved from https://www.pandemicoversight.gov/data-interactive-tools/interactive-dashboards/paycheck-protection-program.

16. Congressional Budget Office.

Chapter 6

1. Federal Reserve Economic Data. FRED.
2. CBS News. (2019, July 9). Ross Perot: The 60 Minutes Interview. Retrieved from https://www.cbsnews.com/news/ross-perot-the-60-minutes-interview-2019-07-09/.
3. Congressional Budget Office.
4. Keynes, J. M. (1919). The Economic Consequences of the Peace.
5. Gladstein, A. $1.2 Billion People Live Under Double-Digit Inflation; Many Have Found Escape in Bitcoin, Says HRF's Alex Gladstein. Bitcoin.com. Retrieved from https://news.bitcoin.com/1-2-billion-people-live-under-double-digit-inflation-many-have-found-escape-in-bitcoin-says-hrfs-alex-gladstein/.
6. NYDIG. (2021). Bitcoin Net Zero. Retrieved from https://assets.website-files.com/614e11526f6630959fc98679/616df63a27a7ec339f5e6a80_NYDIG-BitcoinNetZero_SML.pdf.
7. Alden, L. (2023, November). Retrieved from https://www.lynalden.com/november-2023-newsletter/.
8. Dalio, R. (2021). Changing World Order. Simon & Schuster.
9. The Financial Express. Bangladesh Economy Faces Headwinds. Retrieved from https://thefinancialexpress.com.bd/views/bangladesh-economy-faces-headwinds.
10. Gladstein, A. (2022). Check Your Financial Privilege. BTC Media.

11. Alden, L. (2020). The Fraying of the US Global Currency Reserve System. Retrieved from https://www.lynalden.com/fraying-petrodollar-system/.

12. Center for Strategic & International Studies. Past, Present, and Future of U.S. Assistance to Ukraine: A Deep Dive into Data. Retrieved from https://www.csis.org/analysis/past-present-and-future-us-assistance-ukraine-deep-dive-data.

13. U.S. Department of the Treasury. Retrieved from https://home.treasury.gov/news/press-releases/jy1298.

Chapter 7

1. National Science and Media Museum. A Short History of the Internet. Retrieved from https://www.scienceandmediamuseum.org.uk/objects-and-stories/short-history-internet.

2. Pew Research Center. Internet/Broadband Fact Sheet. Retrieved from https://www.pewresearch.org/internet/fact-sheet/internet-broadband/.

3. Nielsen. (2018, July 31). Time Flies: U.S. Adults Now Spend Nearly Half a Day Interacting with Media. Retrieved from https://www.nielsen.com/insights/2018/time-flies-us-adults-now-spend-nearly-half-a-day-interacting-with-media/.

4. National Academy of Sciences. (2019). Proceedings of the National Academy of Sciences of the United States of America. DOI: 10.1073/pnas.1908630116. Retrieved from https://www.pnas.org/doi/abs/10.1073/pnas.1908630116.

5. Pew Research Center. (2021, January 12). More than eight-in-ten Americans get news from digital devices. Retrieved from https://www.pewresearch.org/short-reads/2021/01/12/more-than-eight-in-ten-americans-get-news-from-digital-devices/.

6. The World Bank. The Global Findex Database. Retrieved from https://www.worldbank.org/en/publication/globalfindex.

7. Pew Research Center. (2022, October 5). More Americans are joining the 'cashless' economy. Retrieved from https://www.pewresearch.org/short-reads/2022/10/05/more-americans-are-joining-the-cashless-economy/.

8. Black, D. (2020, March 1). Who Needs Cryptocurrency FedCoin When We Already Have A National Digital Currency? Forbes. Retrieved from https://www.forbes.com/sites/davidblack/2020/03/01/who-needs-cryptocurrency-fedcoin-when-we-already-have-a-national-digital-currency/?sh=53a4d6644951.

9. Miltimore, J. (2023a, December 18). *Charlie Munger's Rules for Life-in His Own Words*. Foundation for Economic Education. Retrieved from https://fee.org/articles/charlie-mungers-rules-for-life-in-his-own-words/.

10. Hayek, F. (1944). The Road to Serfdom.

11. U.S. Department of the Treasury. Debt Limit. Retrieved from https://home.treasury.gov/policy-issues/financial-markets-financial-institutions-and-fiscal-service/debt-limit.

12. Fox News. FLASHBACK: Treasury Sec. Yellen didn't 'believe' she'd see another financial crisis in her lifetime. Retrieved from

https://www.foxnews.com/politics/flashback-treasury-sec-yellen-didnt-believe-shed-see-another-financial-crisis-in-her-lifetime.

13. National Bureau of Economic Research. (2021, July 19). Business Cycle Dating Committee Announcement. Retrieved from https://www.nber.org/news/business-cycle-dating-committee-announcement-july-19-2021.

14. Rev. (2021, June 22). Jerome Powell Testimony on Fed's Pandemic Response Transcript. Retrieved from https://www.rev.com/blog/transcripts/jerome-powell-testimony-on-feds-pandemic-response-june-22.

15. Bloomberg. (2023, October 5). Bond Traders Wager Historic Sums on November Fed Meeting Outcome. Retrieved from https://www.bloomberg.com/news/articles/2023-10-05/bond-traders-wager-historic-sums-on-november-fed-meeting-outcome.

Chapter 8

1. CNN. (2021, February 24). The Federal Reserve suffers widespread disruption to payment services. Retrieved from https://www.cnn.com/2021/02/24/business/federal-reserve-outage-fedwire/index.html.

2. The New York Times. (2014, January 21). Why Bitcoin Matters. Retrieved from https://archive.nytimes.com/dealbook.nytimes.com/2014/01/21/why-bitcoin-matters/.

3. Electronic Frontier Foundation. Section 230 of the Communications Decency Act. Retrieved from https://www.eff.org/issues/cda230.

4. Yarow, J. (2013, December 30). *Paul Krugman Responds to all the People Throwing Around his Old Internet Quote.* Business Insider. Retrieved from https://www.businessinsider.com/paul-krugman-responds-to-internet-quote-2013-12 .

5. Harvard Business Review. (2013, November). The Pace of Technology Adoption is Speeding Up. Retrieved from https://hbr.org/2013/11/the-pace-of-technology-adoption-is-speeding-up.

6. Bitcoin Wiki. B-money. Retrieved from https://en.bitcoin.it/wiki/B-money.

7. Cord Magazine. Roya Mahboob: Afghan Woman Who Became a Chief Executive at 23. Retrieved from https://cordmagazine.com/business/entrepreneurship/roya-mahboob-afghan-woman-who-became-a-chief-executive-at-23/.

8. Gladstein, A. (2022). Check Your Financial Privilege. BTC Media.

9. Council on Foreign Relations. Venezuela's Crisis. Retrieved from https://www.cfr.org/backgrounder/venezuela-crisis.

10. Rodríguez, Francisco; Iyer, Lakshmi (2021). Hyperinflation in Venezuela. University of Notre Dame. Report. Retrieved from https://doi.org/10.7274/r0-z7wm-f385.

11. Statista. Average inflation rate in Venezuela. Retrieved from https://www.statista.com/statistics/1392610/average-inflation-rate-venezuela/.

12. World Bank.

13. CoinDesk. (2020, November 11). Venezuela's Bitcoin Story Puts It in a Category of One. Retrieved from

https://www.coindesk.com/business/2020/11/11/venezuel as-bitcoin-story-puts-it-in-a-category-of-one/.

14. BTCMap.
15. Chainalysis. (2023). The 2023 Geography of Cryptocurrency Report.
16. Unchained Crypto. 77% of Financial Advisors Are Waiting for a Spot Bitcoin ETF to Offer Their Clients. Retrieved from https://unchainedcrypto.com/77-of-financial-advisors-are-waiting-for-a-spot-bitcoin-etf-to-offer-their-clients/.
17. Crypto.com. (2024, January). Crypto Market Sizing 2023. Retrieved from https://contenthub-static.crypto.com/wp_media/2024/01/Crypto-Market-Sizing-2023.pdf.

Chapter 9

1. Gladstein, A. (2022). Check Your Financial Privilege. BTC Media.
2. International Monetary Fund. Data. Retrieved from https://data.imf.org/regular.aspx?key=41175.
3. Blockworks. El Salvador's Bitcoin bet in green. Retrieved from https://blockworks.co/news/el-salvador-bitcoin-bet-in-green.
4. Sovereign Wealth Fund Institute. Abu Dhabi Sovereign Wealth Funnels Capital into Bitcoin Mining. Retrieved from https://www.swfinstitute.org/news/97212/abu-dhabi-sovereign-wealth-funnels-capital-into-bitcoin-mining.
5. Martin, I. (2023, April 30). Bhutan Bitcoin Mining Crypto. Forbes. Retrieved from

https://www.forbes.com/sites/iainmartin/2023/04/30/bhutan-bitcoin-mining-crypto/?sh=2c0dee081f1b.

6. MassMutual. (2020, December). Institutional Bitcoin Provider NYDIG Announces Minority Stake Purchase by MassMutual. Retrieved from https://www.massmutual.com/about-us/news-and-press-releases/press-releases/2020/12/institutional-bitcoin-provider-nydig-announces-minority-stake-purchase-by-massmutual.

7. CNBC. (2021, February 8). Tesla buys $1.5 billion in bitcoin, plans to accept it as payment. Retrieved from https://www.cnbc.com/2021/02/08/tesla-buys-1point5-billion-in-bitcoin.html.

8. Cointelegraph. Retrieved from https://cointelegraph.com/news/i-d-rather-bitcoin-over-bonds-billionaire-investor-ray-dalio.

9. CoinDesk. (2023, July 5). BlackRock CEO Larry Fink Says Bitcoin Could 'Revolutionize Finance'. Retrieved from https://www.coindesk.com/business/2023/07/05/blackrock-ceo-larry-fink-says-bitcoin-could-revolutionize-finance/.

10. Gall, J. (1975). Systemantics.

11. Connect Brazil. The Story of Brasília. Retrieved from https://www.connectbrazil.com/the-story-of-brasilia/.

12. University of Michigan Library. Brazilianization of Brasília. Retrieved from https://quod.lib.umich.edu/j/jii/4750978.0014.214/--brazilianization-of-brasilia?rgn=main;view=fulltext;q1=Space%2C+Architecture+and+Urban+Studies.

13. Wikimedia Commons. File:Planalto Central (cropped).jpg. Retrieved from https://commons.wikimedia.org/wiki/File:Planalto_Central_(cropped).jpg.

14. University of Texas at Austin. Modernist Architecture and the Failures of Place-Making in Brasília. Retrieved from https://sites.utexas.edu/internationalplanning/case-studies/modernist-architecture-and-the-failures-of-place-making-in-brasilia/.

15. Farrington, A. (2020, May 2). It's Time To Reflect. Medium. https://allenfarrington.medium.com/its-time-to-reflect-21673608f5a1

16. Visa. About Visa - VisaNet Technology. Retrieved from https://www.visa.co.uk/dam/VCOM/download/corporate/media/visanet-technology/aboutvisafactsheet.pdf.

17. Federal Reserve Economic Data. FRED.

18. Coin Metrics.

Chapter 10

1. Gladstein, A. (2022). Check Your Financial Privilege. BTC Media.

2. Africa at LSE. (2019, June 5). The CFA franc: French monetary imperialism in Africa. Retrieved from https://blogs.lse.ac.uk/africaatlse/2017/07/12/the-cfa-franc-french-monetary-imperialism-in-africa/.

3. Pigeaud, F., & Sylla, N. S. (2021). Africa's Last Colonial Currency: The CFA Franc Story. Pluto Press.

4. Brookings. (2022, March 9). How the France-backed African CFA franc works as an enabler and barrier to development. Retrieved from https://www.brookings.edu/articles/how-the-france-

backed-african-cfa-franc-works-as-an-enabler-and-barrier-to-development/.

5. 2023 Index of Economic Freedom. Senegal. Retrieved from https://www.heritage.org/index/country/senegal.

6. Cointelegraph. (2022, March 8). Mama Bitcoin: Fishing for female empowerment with crypto in West Africa. Retrieved from https://cointelegraph.com/news/mama-bitcoin-fishing-for-female-empowerment-with-crypto-in-west-africa.

7. Cointelegraph. (2022b, March 16). "We don't like our money": The story of the CFA and Bitcoin in Africa. Retrieved from https://cointelegraph.com/news/we-don-t-like-our-money-the-story-of-the-cfa-and-bitcoin-in-africa.

8. Boaz Sobrado's Website. (2020, May 22). A day using money in Cuba. Retrieved from https://boazsobrado.com/blog/2020/05/22/a-day-using-money-in-cuba/.

9. Reuters. (2021, July 14). White House may ease ban on remittances as part of Cuba review. Retrieved from https://www.reuters.com/world/americas/white-house-may-ease-ban-remittances-part-cuba-review-sources-2021-07-14/.

10. U.S. Embassy in Cuba. (2019, September 6). United States Restricts Remittances and "U-Turn" Transactions to Cuba. Retrieved from https://cu.usembassy.gov/united-states-restricts-remittances-and-u-turn-transactions-to-cuba/.

11. United Nations. (2019, June 17). Remittances matter: 8 facts you don't know about the money migrants send back home. Retrieved from

https://www.un.org/development/desa/en/news/populatio
n/remittances-matter.html.

12. Knomad. (2023, December) Migration and Development
Brief 39. Retrieved from
https://www.knomad.org/publication/migration-and-
development-brief-39.

13. The World Bank. (2022). Personal remittances, received
(% of GDP). Retrieved from
https://data.worldbank.org/indicator/BX.TRF.PWKR.DT
.GD.ZS?most_recent_value_desc=true.

14. World Bank. (2023, September). Remittance Prices
Worldwide. Retrieved from
https://remittanceprices.worldbank.org/.

15. FSD Ethiopia. (2022). Why Financial Inclusion Matters.
Retrieved from https://fsdethiopia.org/our-work/.

Epilogue

1. Reinhart, C. M., & Rogoff, K. S. (2009). This Time Is
Different: Eight Centuries of Financial Folly.

2. Corporate Finance Institute. Dotcom Bubble. Retrieved
from
https://corporatefinanceinstitute.com/resources/career-
map/sell-side/capital-markets/dotcom-bubble/.

3. Cointelegraph. (2022). Sam Bankman-Fried. Retrieved
from https://cointelegraph.com/top-people-in-crypto-and-
blockchain-2022/sam-bankman-fried.

4. CNBC. (2023, November 4). Sam Bankman-Fried faces
over 100 years in prison at sentencing. Experts weigh in
on how much time he'll actually get. Retrieved from
https://www.cnbc.com/2023/11/04/sam-bankman-fried-
sentence-could-be-100-plus-years-or-mere-decades.html.

5. NYDIG. (2021). Report: Bitcoin Net Zero. Retrieved from https://nydig.com/research/report-bitcoin-net-zero.

6. The Fact Source. How Much Electricity Does YouTube Use? Retrieved from https://thefactsource.com/how-much-electricity-does-youtube-use/.

7. Carter, N., Connell, S., Jones, B., Porter, D., & Rudd, M. (2023, November 22). Leveraging Bitcoin Miners as Flexible Load Resources for Power System Stability and Efficiency. SSRN. Retrieved from https://doi.org/10.2139/ssrn.4634256.

8. Armstrong, D., Scalia, A. (2021). Bitcoin Mining and the Case for More Energy. Retrieved from https://bitcoinmagazine.com/culture/bitcoin-mining-and-the-case-for-more-energy.

9. KPMG. (2023). Bitcoin's Role in The ESG Imperative. Retrieved from https://kpmg.com/us/en/articles/2023/bitcoin-role-esg-imperative.html.

10. Bitcoin Mining Council. (2022). Bitcoin Mining Electricity Mix Increased to 59.5% Sustainable in Q2 2022. Retrieved from https://bitcoinminingcouncil.com/bitcoin-mining-electricity-mix-increased-to-59-5-sustainable-in-q2-2022/.

11. SatoshiAction. Bitcoin Miners Return Enough Power to Heat 1.5 Million Homes During Texas Winter Storm. Retrieved from https://www.satoshiaction.io/post/bitcoin-miners-return-enough-power-to-heat-1-5-million-homes-during-texas-winter-storm.

12. International Man. Can the Government Ban Bitcoin? Four Things You Need to Know Today. Retrieved from https://internationalman.com/articles/can-the-

government-ban-bitcoin-four-things-you-need-to-know-today/.

13. CoinDesk. (2021, July 6). Thriving Under Pressure: Why Crypto Is Booming in Nigeria Despite the Banking Ban. Retrieved from https://www.coindesk.com/markets/2021/07/06/thriving-under-pressure-why-crypto-is-booming-in-nigeria-despite-the-banking-ban/.

14. CoinDesk. (2023, December 27). Nigeria Lifting Ban on Bank Accounts for Crypto Firms Could Lead to Usage Surge. Retrieved from https://www.coindesk.com/policy/2023/12/27/nigeria-lifting-ban-on-bank-accounts-for-crypto-firms-could-lead-to-usage-surge/.

15. Bitcoin.com News. Finder Survey: Nigeria's 24.2% Adoption Rating Is the Highest Rate of Crypto Ownership Globally. Retrieved from https://news.bitcoin.com/finder-survey-nigerias-24-2-adoption-rating-is-the-highest-rate-of-crypto-ownership-globally/.

16. Roy, A. (2021). Bitcoin and the US Fiscal Reckoning. National Affairs. Retrieved from https://nationalaffairs.com/publications/detail/bitcoin-and-the-us-fiscal-reckoning.

17. Fidelity Digital Assets. Addressing Persisting Bitcoin Criticisms. Retrieved from https://www.fidelitydigitalassets.com/research-and-insights/addressing-persisting-bitcoin-criticisms.

18. Better Markets. Wall Street's Rap Sheet: 6 Biggest Banks Rack Up Another $9 Billion in Fines. Retrieved from

https://bettermarkets.org/newsroom/wall-streets-rap-sheet-6-biggest-banks-rack-up-another-9-billion-in-fines.

19. Global Investigations Review. Money Laundering Through Digital Assets. Retrieved from https://globalinvestigationsreview.com/guide/the-guide-anti-money-laundering/first-edition/article/money-laundering-through-digital-assets.

GLOSSARY

Bailout: Financial support to prevent bankruptcy.

Banknote: Paper money issued by a bank.

Bitcoin Mining: The process of validating transactions and securing the Bitcoin network.

Bitcoin Wallet: The term used for the physical or digital device that stores bitcoin. Specifically, a bitcoin wallet stores the keys (password) used to access bitcoin.

Blockchain: A decentralized ledger of all transactions distributed across a network.

Bond: A fixed income investment representing a loan made by an investor to a borrower.

Budget Deficit: The shortfall when a government's spending exceeds revenue.

Central Bank Reserves: Deposits held by central banks as a reserve.

Central Banks: Institutions that manage a state's currency, money supply, and interest rates.

CFA Franc: The CFA Franc is a currency used in 14 African countries, divided into two regions: West Africa and Central Africa, each with its own version of the CFA Franc. It is guaranteed by the French treasury and was originally pegged to the French Franc but is now pegged to the Euro. The CFA Franc aims to provide currency stability for its member countries. The acronym CFA stands for "Communauté Financière Africaine" in West Africa and "Coopération Financière en Afrique Centrale" in Central Africa, reflecting the currency's role in financial cooperation and integration within these regions.

Commodity Money: Money whose value comes from a commodity of which it is made, such as cowrie shells, gold, and tobacco.

Cryptocurrency: Digital or virtual currency using cryptography for security.

Cryptography: Cryptography is a field of computer science that studies how to securely communicate in the presence of potential adversaries. In the Bitcoin network, cryptography is used to secure transactions and control the creation of new units. It employs cryptographic algorithms for digital signatures and hash functions to ensure the integrity and authenticity of transactions. For example, Bitcoin's blockchain uses the SHA-256 hash function to create a secure and immutable record of transactions.

CUC: The Cuban Convertible Peso (CUC) was a currency used in Cuba alongside the Cuban Peso

(CUP). The CUC was pegged to the US dollar and was introduced in 1994 as a part of the dual currency system to facilitate the exchange of foreign currencies. It was primarily used in the tourism sector and for luxury goods, while the Cuban Peso was used for domestic transactions and salaries.

The CUC was valued at a higher rate than the CUP, creating a disparity in purchasing power within the country. This dual system was intended to protect the domestic economy from fluctuations in foreign currencies and to help manage Cuba's economic challenges. However, it also led to complexities and inequalities in the economy.

As part of economic reforms aimed at unifying the dual currency system, the Cuban government announced the phasing out of the CUC, with the goal of simplifying transactions and reducing economic distortions. The process towards devaluation and eventual elimination of the CUC has been underway, with the Cuban Peso (CUP) set to become the sole currency for all transactions within the country.

Currency: Currency refers to money in any form when in use or circulation as a medium of exchange, especially circulating banknotes and coins.

Devaluation / Debasement: Devaluation refers to the reduction in value of a currency via money printing. Debasement refers to reducing the value of a coinage by lowering the content of precious metals. An example is when the Roman Empire debased their silver coins to fund the empire, leading to inflation.

Digital Native: A "digitally native" currency, like Bitcoin, is designed exclusively for the digital ecosystem, utilizing cryptographic techniques to secure transactions, control the creation of new units, and verify asset transfers. Unlike traditional currencies, which evolved from physical to digital forms, Bitcoin was conceived as digital-first, enabling peer-to-peer transactions without the need for central authorities, illustrating a revolutionary approach to money in the digital age.

Dunbar's Number: A theoretical cognitive limit to the number of people with whom one can maintain stable social relationships.

Executive Order 6102: Issued in 1933 by President Franklin D. Roosevelt, this order required U.S. citizens to exchange their gold coins, bullion, and certificates for U.S. dollars to combat banking panics and the Great Depression. It essentially outlawed the possession of monetary gold by any individual, partnership, association, or corporation.

Fiat Money: Currency without intrinsic value established as money by government regulation.

Fiscal Stimulus: Increased government spending or tax reductions to encourage economic growth.

Gall's Law: A complex system that works is invariably found to have evolved from a simple system that worked.

GDP: A standard measure for the size of an economy. Specifically, Gross Domestic Product is a monetary measure of the market value of all the final goods and services produced in a specific time period.

Gold Convertibility: Gold convertibility is the feature of a currency system where the currency can be exchanged for a specific amount of gold. For example, under the Bretton Woods system post-World War II, many currencies were pegged to the U.S. dollar, which was convertible to gold at a fixed rate.

Gold Standard: A monetary system where currency or paper money has a value directly linked to gold.

Government Bond: A debt security issued by a government to support government spending.

Hyperinflation: Extremely rapid or out-of-control inflation, defined as a monthly inflation rate exceeding 50%.

Inflation: The rate at which the general level of prices for goods and services is rising.

Intermediary: A middleman or agent between two parties participating in a transaction.

MLC: In Cuba, MLC stands for "Moneda Libremente Convertible," which translates to "Freely Convertible Currency." The MLC system was introduced as part of economic reforms aimed at addressing the shortage of foreign currency within the country. The MLC operates alongside the Cuban Peso (CUP), serving as a mechanism for transactions involving foreign currencies.

Under the MLC system, certain goods and services can only be purchased with a form of payment that is equivalent to foreign currency, such as bank transfers or cards charged with foreign currencies. This system is primarily used in special stores and for specific services where transactions are conducted in or equivalent to foreign currencies, rather than in the traditional Cuban Peso.

The introduction of the MLC system has significant implications for the Cuban economy, including the way Cubans and visitors conduct transactions, the accessibility of certain goods, and the overall economic strategy of the Cuban government to stabilize foreign currency reserves and improve the import of essential goods.

Monetary policy: Monetary policy involves the management of a nation's money supply and interest rates by its central bank to control inflation, stabilize currency, foster economic growth, and reduce unemployment. For example, the Federal Reserve may stimulate the economy by introducing new money into the system, via a process known as "quantitative easing".

Monetary Stimulus: Central bank measures to increase money supply to boost the economy.

Path Dependence: Path dependence is the idea that the present state of a technology or system results from the cumulative impact of historical, pragmatic decisions made along the path of its development

Proof-of-work: Proof-of-Work is a mechanism used by Bitcoin to validate transactions and create new blocks on the blockchain. Miners solve complex mathematical problems, and the first to solve the problem gets to add a new block to the blockchain, receiving Bitcoin as a reward for their efforts.

Purchasing Power: The value of a currency expressed in terms of the amount of goods or services that one unit of money can buy.

Remittances: Money sent by a person in one country to a person in another country.

Reserve Currency: A currency that is held in significant quantities by governments and institutions as part of their foreign exchange reserves.

Satoshi Nakamoto: The pseudonymous person or group of people who developed Bitcoin.

Speculation: The practice of engaging in risky financial transactions in an attempt to profit from short or medium-term fluctuations.

The Bretton Woods System: A monetary management system that established the rules for commercial and financial relations among the United States, Canada, Western European countries, Australia, and Japan after the 1944 Bretton Woods Agreement.

The Federal Reserve: The central bank of the United States.

The Lightning Network: A "second layer" payment protocol that operates on top of Bitcoin to enable faster transactions.

Trade Balance: The difference between a country's exports and imports.

US Treasury: The department of the US government responsible for issuing all Treasury bonds, notes, and bills.

VOC (Dutch East India Company): A historical megacorporation founded by a government-directed consolidation of several rival Dutch trading companies in the early 17th century.

Volatility: The degree of variation of a trading price series over time.